1984

Your Emotional Life and What You Can Do About It

Your Emotional Life and What You Can Do About It

by James F. Drane

THE THOMAS MORE PRESS
Chicago, Illinois

ISBN 0-88347-157-4

Grateful acknowledgment to the following for permission to quote copyrighted material:

Karl Menninger, *The Human Mind.* Copyright © 1973 by Karl Menninger. Used by permission of Alfred A. Knopf, N.Y., N.Y.

Karl Menninger, *The Vital Balance.* Copyright © 1963 by Karl Menninger. Used by permission of The Viking Press, N.Y., N.Y.

Contents

Introduction, 9

I. UNDERSTANDING HUMAN FEELINGS

   1. Feelings that make us well, 18
   2. Feelings that make us ill, 24
   3. Funny things that cause emotional problems, 30
   4. Who are the doctors for these problems, 34
   5. Interesting facts about emotions, 40
   6. Understanding unusual behavior, 46
   7. Personalities twisted by threatening feelings, 59
   8. People who drive other people crazy, 74
   9. People dangerous to others and to themselves, 77
 10. Aloof, detached, and terrified personalities, 84

II. LEVELS OF HEALTHY AND UNHEALTHY
FUNCTIONING

   1. Healthy emotional life—a matter of smart tactics, 90
   2. Ineffectual responses to normal disruptions—forgetting, overworking, substituting, worrying, fantasizing, getting sick: Level I, 98
   3. Withdrawal and the beginning of more serious forms of emotional illness—fainting, amnesia, fugue states, prejudice, fantasies, phobias: Level II, 102
   4. Care and its absence in second-level forms of distress, 107
   5. Not caring for others—symbolic killing, revenge, self righteousness, 109
   6. Not caring for oneself—mutilation, substance abuse, and depression, 113

7. Unusual strategies for managing aggression and hostilities—compulsions and sexual perversions, 117
8. A further deterioration of emotional health—violent crime, battering, assault, rage: Level III, 124
9. Full-blown forms of insanity—depression, mania, schizophrenia, paranoia: Level IV, 131
10. Suicide, the ultimate in flawed coping devices: Level V, 146

III. COPING WITH PAINFUL FEELINGS
1. Thinking and talking about feelings, 153
2. Feeling conflicted, 161
3. Feeling depressed, 166
4. Feeling anxious, 171
5. Feeling spiteful, 177
6. Feeling shame or guilt, 182
7. Feeling angry, 189
8. Feeling useless, 191
9. Feeling worried, 193
10. Feeling bored, 198

Notes, 203

FOREWORD

THIS book is about emotions, particularly negative ones like anger, hostility, aggression, and the devices people use to manage them. It uses psychiatric and religious sources and tries to present this material so that ordinary people can better understand themselves and even help themselves when they feel upset. Why? Because emotional problems are on the increase, and one of the best ways of managing them is through understanding.

Understanding not only cures but prevents emotional illness from occurring in the first place. As soon as a person sees with some clarity his behavioral patterns or personality traits, or has a better grasp of his feeling states, he gains power over them. Seeing and understanding are pre-conditions for healthy change.

Anyone familiar with the work of Karl Menninger will recognize the major source of the ideas expressed here. The overall model for understanding feelings and human coping devices, I learned from him. And it was his interest in getting psychiatric information passed on to ordinary people which influenced me to write this little book.

J.F.D.

For Theresa, Phil, Mark, Lynn, and Jon, who have forced me to abandon some ineffective coping devices and helped me to develop some better management techniques.

* * *

The work on this book was done at the Baron-Forness Library of Edinboro University of Pennsylvania. Many persons there helped me. Special thanks are due to Connie Downey, Kay Petrusky, and Saul Weinstein.

INTRODUCTION

THIS is a book about the feelings which are part of every life. It is a book about devices and techniques used to cope with feelings. Finally, it is a book about happy people and about people who live their lives in misery.

These three themes are interrelated. We adapt to changing situations by developing regulatory devices for our emotions. These devices either help us to keep our balance and therefore to enjoy a satisfying life or they fail to do so. Happiness (and unhappiness) has a lot to do with our predominant feelings, but it is even more a matter of the way we handle feelings. We human beings have always been aware of the emotional dimension of our lives, but recently have we learned to identify techniques used to cope with emotions and to distinguish those which contribute to health from those which cause illness and misery.

1. Feelings

Feelings provide the tone of life, and it is all too obvious that a positive feeling tone is closely connected to happiness. But feelings seem to be beyond our control. One of the truisms of our times is that "we cannot help how we feel." Are some of us then simply condemned to be unhappy because we cannot help having unhappy feelings? I don't think so. As long as we do not understand our feelings, they will surely have free rein and rule us more than we rule them. But understanding produces a magical form of mastery. We'll never completely dominate our feelings (and wouldn't want to), but we can and should gain a measure of control over the affective part of our lives; and as we do, our chance of attaining a modest amount of happiness is considerably enhanced.

Some blessed people have a natural abundance of positive feelings. They have happy dispositions, smile easily, and are not given to brooding when things go wrong. Others are not so naturally blessed, but have learned to work on their feelings and to modify the worst of them. They don't let things get them down. Even in the midst of hurtful events, they are able to think themselves into more positive feeling states and manage to keep the tone of their lives mainly on the positive side. Happiness is often a matter of spending time and effort in the pursuit of healthy satisfaction instead of waiting for luck or chance to make us happy. Working on happiness and good feelings, however, can be overdone. No one can consistently keep his feelings positive, and the more one tries to force good feelings, the more elusive they become.

Is it worth trying to improve the way we feel? Certainly it is. We can bring ourselves out of black moods and negative feelings. And there is a sense in which we can create positive emotions by setting out to feel good. Trying to force feelings is one thing, but working to improve an emotional state is a different and altogether sensible project. Feelings are worth working on because they influence the world in which we live. The world of a person dominated by down feelings is bleak and stark. For the person who is afraid, it is threatening and suspicious. The angry person's world is full of obstacles and delays. For the sad person, or for one who feels sick, the world is too powerful to manage. Joy, on the other hand, works a magic and makes the world an easy place to be in. Feelings are worth working on because they not only connect us to the world, but transform the world for us.

But how do we go about such a project? Our culture certainly is not much help. It has produced a highly refined vocabulary for the physical dimensions of reality, but ask even a well-educated person to describe his feelings and see what a difficulty this creates. Or ask someone to discriminate among related but different feelings and notice how quickly he becomes tongue-tied. Whether we don't have words for feelings or have lost command of them is hard to decide. American males especially are taught to repress feelings, and any weakening of repressive mechanisms is taken to be a sign of weakness. Emotions shown publicly can disqualify a completely competent person from high political, economic, or even ecclesiastical office. No wonder we know so little about emotions. It's almost against the law to have them.

In the third and final section of the book we'll look into some of the more common feeling states, learn how to distinguish one from another, and see what effect different emotions have on our lives. We'll try to get smarter about our feelings. In the first and second sections we will focus on those feelings which are the most elusive and at the same time the most destructive of happiness: emotions like anger, aggression, hostility. Unless we understand these negative feelings better, even a minimal amount of happiness will elude us. Instead of being happy, we will be the victims of both emotional and physical illness.

2. Coping Devices

Besides taking a closer look at the feelings we all experience, we will give a lot of attention in this book to the ways people manage their feelings. Emotions are elusive but nowhere near as difficult to grasp as the behaviors we use to handle them. Human beings from the dawn of history have commented upon feelings, and sometimes very perceptively. But only in the last split second of evolutionary time have we even recognized the different coping strategies people use for managing feelings. Now, however, anyone can learn to recognize strategies, and once we do so both the feeling states and our standard ways of responding to them can be changed. Life will never be dominated or forced totally within our grasp, but we can have more control than we think, even over our feeling states. Getting smart about emotions includes learning about standard coping devices to which they are linked.

The most important devices are those connected to the negative emotions. There is no way of avoiding either upsets or their associated feelings, but there are ways of avoiding the worst ways of handling them. Just knowing about bad strategies and being able to recognize them in ourselves and others constitutes a giant step toward developing better strategies. Some coping devices are smart and efficient and help us over the rough spots in the road. Others are dumb and inefficient and only compound our troubles. Especially these latter we need to know about in order to avoid or at least to use only infrequently. Healthy and happy lives are a matter of some good feelings and some sound strategies for handling the bad ones.

Coping devices for the emotional side of life are like physical or organic coping devices. Change takes place in the body which upsets its physical balance, and the body begins to employ defense strategies. It increases the body temperature (fever), sends nerve signals to sound an alert (pain), accumulates blood around the areas of upset (swelling), and so on. When these coping devices are on target, equilibrium is quickly restored. Physical health is not a matter of avoiding germs and injuries, but more a matter of having an effective system of defenses and devices for handling them. The same is true of emotional health. Emotional upsets in the form of disrupted personal relations or confused thoughts generate strong negative emotions. Emotional coping strategies follow emotional upsets. If these are effective, a healthy emotional balance will be soon restored. Otherwise, the upsets continue, and associated negative emotions pollute our lives. For both physical and emotional health, we need coping devices and defense mechanisms which are not too costly and which work efficiently to keep our lives in balance.

Let me offer an example. A misunderstanding or perhaps a difference of opinion occurs with someone we care about. Painful emotions are created. Some handle these feelings by turning them back on themselves. Other people let them out in bursts of anger. Still others hold them in, creating migraine headaches and digestive disorders. It makes good sense for each person to try to learn what kind of coping devices he uses. Ignorance means being condemned to the unhappiness associated with the worst strategies. Understanding, on the other hand, means a chance to substitute a more efficient for a less efficient strategy. Understanding, in effect, makes it possible to grow, to mature, and consequently to derive some happiness from life.

A degree of satisfaction or a sense of gratitude for the gift of life is not just for the lucky people who have been spared major upsets, but for the smart ones who have found the healthiest coping devices for managing feelings. The same awful feelings that lead to unhappiness or even sickness can be turned into pearls of growth, strength, and self-esteem when they are effectively handled. Some who have had all kinds of misfortunes turn out to be beautiful people. Others who have had the same misfortunes turn out to be real "pains." No one knows why people turn out so differently, but we can know which ways of managing feelings are characteristic of the "pains" and which typify the attractive people. Once we learn to recognize the good and bad coping devices, we can begin to nourish the good ones in ourselves and to change the ineffective ones. It makes sense to pay attention to persistent feelings, especially the negative ones, and to the devices we use to manage them. Learning about feelings and strategies can mean the difference between a life trapped in unhappiness and a life which grows, enjoys, learns, works productively, and has loving relationships.

3. *Happiness*

No one would deny that there are elements of luck in happiness, but it is never just a matter of luck. Happiness to some extent at least, is the fruit of efforts to find the keys to happiness. First of all, it is a matter of learning to avoid the worst stumbling blocks and obstacles to real satisfaction.

On the more positive side it is a matter of learning about feelings and the most effective strategies for managing them. We can learn to play and work, to pray and do good things for others, just as we can learn to avoid depression, revenge, and forms of self-hurting. As soon as we recognize what pain we are causing ourselves by using the worst coping devices, we have taken a giant step toward changing them. The sad and pitiful people, for example, who wallow in depression or who sit alone in bars drinking themselves into oblivion usually have not learned better ways of handling their feelings. Somewhere along the line they got stuck in the use of happiness-destroying strategies. Delinquent kids, too, provide examples of using ineffective coping strategies for the management of feelings which rob life of its satisfactions. Helping the delinquent is an educational process, a matter of learning life-enhancing rather than life-destroying coping strategies.

There are events in life that cause intense and sometimes terrifying emotions, but these do not usually create lasting unhappiness. The death of a parent, for example, will cause a flood of terrifying emotions and undoubtedly influence a child. If the parent had not died, without doubt, things would have been different. However, such sad events, and the accompanying sad emotions, do not condemn a young life to unhappiness. Not isolated events and emotions, but those continuing interactions with other people, along with their emotional colorings, make the big difference. The loss of a parent can sidetrack a child for a while, but children usually recover without suffering long-term consequences. Not so, however, with the ambivalent relationship with a parent which goes on for years and is accompanied by less intense, but continuing, negative feelings. These can ruin a life because children do not have available to them a selection of mature coping devices and consequently choose bad strategies for managing their feelings. Gradually, the bad strategies become part of the child's character. If the strategies used are very costly and very ineffective, they make the child downright miserable.

The same principle holds for adults. Even if happiness is never achieved, at least the worst form of unhappiness can be avoided. The most common forms of unhappiness in adults do not come from isolated bits of bad luck, but from ongoing struggles with recurring negative feelings. Unhappiness is due to unsuccessful coping strategies, and it persists because the unsuccessful strategies are never recognized for what they are. Some of the things we spend time on and invest energy in are not worth it. Bad strategies constitute a waste of time and energy. It makes sense, however, to take some time to examine the way we handle upsets and bad feelings. We are all responsible for the quality of our lives. Most unhappiness results from not taking the time to understand the dumb and unproductive way we manage our feelings.

Learning about feelings and the different ways of coping

with them has another big advantage. We cannot use our improved understanding to change other people, but we can become more understanding of their behavior. Our natural tendency is to take what others do and say to us at face value. When what they do hurts us we respond with hurting behavior of our own. Once we learn about the feelings which lie behind people's behavior, however, and learn to recognize their behavior as a more-or-less effective coping device, we can restrain our natural instinct. This gives us the time to fashion a different response. We need not always respond with tit-for-tat, and this is the beginning of a new level of functioning: a more mature and potentially happier way of life.

Martin Luther King, for example, was a person who seemed to be able to respond differently even to very angry and hostile people. Their behavior did not elicit from him the "natural" reaction. He seemed to understand poor white bigots, to see behind their awful coping devices to the terrible feelings they harbored, and finally to the life events which generated them. He was able to not respond in kind to their bitterness and their insults. Understanding gave him an edge. It made his life not only more edifying, but actually happier. It is a mystery how some people develop the coping devices which make their lives so much better off. But everyone can make some improvement just by learning more about feelings and ways of coping with them.

Some people think that they cannot change, but they are mistaken. Change comes in lives at the least expected times. We know about the changes that take place between ages 1 and 5, 5 and 10, 10 and 16, and again between 16 and 21. But there are similar discontinuities in the lives of adults as well. The key to these seemingly mysterious shifts is more often better understanding than biological development. Once a person understands his feelings and his coping devices, he is poised for change. Better understanding improves professional performance, marriages, and friendships.

The mystery is why we cultivate ignorance of the feeling dimension of life in American culture. Why do we spend time learning about things but not about ourselves? Why don't young people learn about the negative feelings that kill and about the positive ones that heal? Why are there no courses about coping skills? Why is it that themes like happiness, friendliness, gentleness, and the like, are not a matter of instruction?

This book is about all these themes. It is never too late to learn.

I. UNDERSTANDING HUMAN FEELINGS

1. Feelings that make us well

In 1976 an unusual article appeared in the *New England Journal of Medicine,* possibly the most prestigious of the medical journals. Most of the articles in the journal are written by physicians and medical researchers and exude an air of scientific seriousness with their data printouts and charts. The unusual article was written by a layman with a background in the humanities rather than science and looked like something which one would find in the *Saturday Review of Literature.* The author, in fact, was the editor of the *Saturday Review.* A medical journal would be the last place in the world to expect to see an article by Norman Cousins, and yet his strange little essay caused an uproar in the medical community.

Entitled, "The Anatomy of an Illness," Cousins' article was the story of his own awful ordeal with a life-threatening illness called ankylosing spondylitis which cripples the person before it kills. The odds against Cousins' survival were 500 to 1. As the disease progressed, he had considerable difficulty moving any part of his body. Nodules appeared in different places and gravel-like substances developed under the skin. At one point, his jaws almost locked. The specialist who diagnosed the disease said that in his long experience, he had never seen a cure.

Recovering from ankylosing spondylitis itself was unusual enough, but the way recovery took place qualifies as astounding. When given the bad news about his condition, Cousins decided that he had to get involved in the medical treatment rather than passively observing the increasingly futile efforts of the medical professionals to help him. Cousins first thought through the events which preceded his falling ill and developed a tentative hypothesis about how the illness started. Then he developed a treatment plan which set out to reverse the factors which had contributed to the problem. The article caused a sensation because what followed was very strange and yet strangely convincing.

Cousins had just returned from an exhausting trip to the Soviet Union when he started to feel ill. The stay in Russia had been full of frustrations. The accompanying negative emotions had not only exhausted him, but weakened his resistance to different sorts of pollution to which he had been exposed. This combination of factors he felt gave the disease process its foothold. Negative emotions he knew affected body functioning, including the endocrine system. Hans Selye, a Canadian researcher in his now classic work, *The Stress of Life*, had shown how negative emotions like frustrations and rage cause severe changes in the body's chemistry, especially in the adrenal gland. Cousins remembered reading Selye's work, and he remembered how improved functioning of the adrenal gland in pregnant women often caused an improvement in arthritic and rheumatic conditions which were similar to his disease. It stood to reason, he thought, that reduced functioning of this crucial gland could have caused his problems and that improving its function could relieve it.

Cousins' logic was straightforward. Negative emotions had caused the problem, positive emotions ought to cure it. If negative emotions produce negative chemical changes in the body, positive emotions ought to produce positive chemical changes. We know that disease and illness of every sort is associated with negative feelings; why isn't the reverse also true? Cousins now had his hypothesis, and from it he fashioned a theory about his disease and how to cure it.

Manipulation of the emotions, however, is not as easy as swallowing a powerful pill. But we do have some control over our emotions, and Cousins reasoned that if only he could get control over his continuing fear, anger, frustration, and hostility, he would take an important step toward improvement. Many of his negative feelings were associated with the hospital environment and standard medical treatment for his illness. So the first step in reversing these feelings was to get out of the hospital. This he did with the blessing of his understanding physician.

The hospital routine had kept his frustration level high and often caused him to be angry. He hated the food, rebelled at having blood drawn three and four times a day, and was convinced that most of the medications he was receiving were poisoning him. Just getting away from this setting would mean a relief from many negative feelings.

The place to which he moved was a comfortable hotel room with a nice view. In this new location he regained some control over his environment. He could order from the restaurant whatever he wanted to eat and the food was good. Besides he was now paying only one-half the price of the hospital room and immediately he started to feel a little better. Next he substituted Vitamin C for all the powerful drugs he had been taking and found that after massive doses of this innocuous vitamin, a lowering of the sedimentation rate occurred—an important indication of improvement. These two changes alone swung his emotion quickly into the positive range. "Seldom," he said, "had I known such elation."

But how does someone keep such positive emotions going? No one can stay elated. If emotions had caused the illness in the first place, it was essential that the positive feelings be turned on and kept on. A strong-minded man, Cousins worked on himself to keep up the positive feelings of hope and love and trust. And then he hit on a way of engineering these feelings. Allen Funt's show, "Candid Camera," had always given him a laugh (it was also my very favorite show and for the same reason). So, he ordered the "Candid Camera" classics, set up a projector and started viewing. Then came another fantastic discovery. A good old-fashioned belly-laugh gave him relief of pain and enabled him to get a couple hours of beneficial pain-free sleep. On awakening, he would look at another film and start the process again. Interspersed with this exercise were readings from a collection of humor books.

But can someone cure a deadly disease just by laughing? Were there any other benefits to the body coming from the positive emotions? Logically, Cousins thought there ought to be. If the negative emotions cause widespread destruction, the positive ones ought to do just the opposite. If the negative emotions through negative change in the glands and body chemistry cause illness, then the positive emotions through positive changes in the body's chemistry ought to cure and heal. Does the body follow this simple Aristotelean logic?

Cousins checked his sedimentation rate before and then after a long happy session full of laughter and again to his pleasant astonishment found that the sedimentation rate dropped another few points. This one indicator, which had gone well over 100 at the worst time of his illness, had been forced down by vitamins and positive emotions. He was proving old theories about laughter being good for the health.

Before long the man who weeks before had been in a hospital awaiting death with an incurable illness was able to move parts of his body without pain. Progress was slow but real. First he was able to stand, then to walk around, finally to get outside the hotel. Later on he got out on the beach, into the water, and finally started to jog for short periods. Norman Cousins finally went back to work. Gradually he went back to playing tennis, and even to playing the piano. This was the amazing story which the editor of the *New England Journal of Medicine* thought should be brought to the attention of the medical community.

The response from that community was almost as astounding as the story itself. "This case proves nothing" was a common reaction. "Realistic conclusions cannot be drawn from one case." "He would have gotten better in any event." "Neither the Vitamin C, nor the positive emotions had any effect on the outcome." These were the most common comments in the flood of mail that followed the article.

Other respondents thought the benefit derived from the Vitamin C and positive emotions came from a placebo effect. The remedies he used had no real effect on his disease it was said, but he felt better because he believed that they were helping him. But did this patient just think he was better while the body went on degenerating from the disease process? No, obviously Cousins became better. If placebo effect means that positive emotions have a stimulating effect on the body's own powers to cure, then that may be the partial or the total explanation of his astounding recovery. Whether the Vitamin C had therapeutic value or whether all the therapy came from the positive emotions would be hard to decide. But Cousins' hypothesis was borne out in objective data. His sediment rate did drop, and the awful arthritis did disappear.

Cousins' thesis about the effect of positive and negative emotions on health receives further support from history. The purely physical effects of most of the medications and therapies provided by physicians throughout history have been antitherapeutic and not just untherapeutic. From a purely physical perspective the bleedings, purges, and emetics which were standard therapies into the nineteenth century had a devastating effect on the body. And yet many people were helped because they *believed* that their situation was understood by the physician and trusted that things would improve from his hands. Rather than wallowing in negative feelings of hopelessness and anger, they became more hopeful and trusting. These positive feelings by themselves had a positive effect on the body's chemistry and ultimately on the illness itself. It may not be too much to say that the history of medicine (before the twentieth century) is a history of the placebo effect. Bleedings, leeches, and purges, emetics did help because through them feelings changed, and with these changes all sorts of other positive effects occurred. People today who receive placebos in controlled studies oftentimes show more physical improvement than those who are taking powerful drugs. Why? The answer seems obvious and incontrovertible. Emotions release powerful forces within the body, especially in the body's own system for fighting disease. Feelings have the power to do either great good or great harm.

Cousins was convinced at the time he was administering Vitamin C that it had a therapeutic value on his collagen disease. It is quite possible that the benefit derived and objectively recorded was a demonstration of the placebo effect. If so, it is an even more convincing witness to the power of positive and negative emotions. Surely some of the miraculous cures of religion fall into this category. And we need no arguments to be convinced that powerful negative emotions cause disease and death. People die of broken hearts, disappointments, loneliness, and frustration. Others get physical and mental illness from the same negative emotions.

Modern medicine has made great advances and has developed a powerful arsenal of weapons for fighting disease. But the more powerful medicine's weapons, the more lopsided medicine becomes. An arsenal of weapons is used to do things to the body. Man's physical nature is treated as a machine which is worked on like a car. Mechanics tend to be quiet types. They don't have to talk to cars. Doctors, too, tend to be quiet. Those who leave off talking and "just treat the body" ignore the emotional side of human beings. They work on people but do not elicit the "doctor within" which is activated by positive emotions.

Hope, love, faith, trust, and humor not only make people feel better, they actually make people better. We cannot always be our own doctor (sometimes this is the height of foolishness), but we do carry a "doctor" within, and emotions either give this healing power a chance to work or stifle it. Feelings are the accelerators or the brakes of our therapeutic motors.

2. Feelings that make us ill

Negative emotions had contributed to the development of a collagen disease in Cousin's case, but these same emotions cause a host of other disorders. How many people do you know who suffer from gastrointestinal disorders which are obviously related to negative emotions like fear, anger, and distrust? Obesity in some people can be traced to emotions no less than the opposite disorder called anorexia nervosa (both of which, by the way, are currently found in epidemic numbers on college campuses). Cardiovascular disorders, respiratory illness, skin problems, arthritis, headaches, can all be caused by negative emotions. People suffering from these problems don't think they are ill. They have real illnesses caused by feelings.

Feelings, however, cause other forms of illness, variously

talked about as emotional problems, emotional illnesses, or emotional afflictions. These are not physical problems like arthritis or a headache, but have a physical component. Emotional illnesses manifest themselves in hurtful behaviors which are the physical symptoms of these illnesses, and they have always been with us. We can find examples of them in both the Old and the New Testament. The following paragraph from St. Mark provides a good example of the type of problem we are referring to.

> And they came to the other side of the sea, to the country of the Gerasenes; and as soon as He stepped out of the boat, there met Him from the tombs a man with an unclean spirit. This man lived in the tombs and no one could any longer bind him, even with chains, for often he had been bound with fetters and chains, and he had rent the chains asunder and broken the fetters into pieces. And no one was able to control him. And constantly, night and day, he was in the tombs and on the mountains, howling and gashing himself with stones (Chapt. 5, 1-5, RSV).

The condition of this poor man was described and understood by the evangelist in religious terms. The disciples of Jesus, following Jewish custom, referred to him as "a man with an unclean spirit." Their terminology is no longer familiar to us, but the behavior is not at all unfamiliar. Howling or crying out is still seen in what we call an emotional breakdown. And the business of gashing or hurting oneself remains one of the hallmarks of what we refer to as serious emotional illness.

A friend of mine, who happened to be a truck driver, found himself under increasing pressure from problems at home, declining health, and job insecurity. More and more frequently he howled, cried, and shouted, not in the hills, but in local bars and other public places. He bruised himself, too, with toxic doses of alcohol and gashed himself with one accident after another. No one could control him either. There was, in fact, very little difference between the self-destructive behavior of the man in the gospel and my friend. And it would not be difficult to cite other cases in which the crying out and self-destruction took exactly the same form as that described by St. Mark. At the time of Jesus there were no cures for such problems available. (The popular idea that, once afflicted by emotional disorder, always afflicted, comes from centuries of experience of helplessness.) In this context, what Jesus did caused astonishment and fear.

> And Jesus immediately gave them leave. And the unclean spirits came out and entered into the swine; and the herd, in number about two thousand, rushed down with great violence into the sea, and were drowned in the sea. But the swineherds fled and reported it in the town and in the country; and people came out to see what had happened. And they came to Jesus, saw the man who had been afflicted by the devil, sitting clothed and in his right mind; and they were afraid (verses 13-15).

Today that unfortunate man would have been taken to a medical facility, diagnosed in medical terms by medical personnel, and started on a series of treatments which most likely would have led to a happy ending. The self-destructive behaviors would be described as symptoms and understood as coping devices for adapting to painful conflict. My friend, for example, was diagnosed in just this way, and after some months of treatment was able to return to work. What Jesus did was miraculous, but now cures which take longer are commonplace.

How does a human being become emotionally disturbed?

What feelings cause a person to become emotionally troubled. What generates the feelings which then cause the destructive symptom of emotional distress? A simple analogy provides us with a starting point for the explanation of this complicated and always somewhat mysterious occurrence. "When a trout rising to a fly gets hooked on a line and finds himself unable to swim about freely, he begins to fight which results in struggle and splashes and sometimes an escape. Often, of course, the situation is too tough for him. In the same way the human being struggles with his environment and with the hooks that catch him. His struggles are all that the world sees, and it usually misunderstands them. It's hard for a free fish to understand what is happening to a hooked one."[1]

The image of a hooked fish is one we all recognize, and it is better than thousands of explanatory words for getting a quick initial insight into emotional affliction. The emotionally afflicted person first feels hooked or trapped by something which happens in life and makes gestures which everyone else judges to be strange. People on the outside see only the odd behaviors. They have no way of seeing what makes the person resort to them. If the hidden hooks (the upsets, the unresolvable conflicts) are deep and particularly painful, then the struggle will be violent. It is the struggling and the violent behaviors which constitute an emotional illness. These behaviors provide a person with an entrance ticket to health-care facilities and to the privileged status of patient.

For one person the struggling and violent behavior will take the form of angrily striking out at innocent victims who happen to be at hand when the feelings of being hooked reach their high point. Indiscriminate violence may reach the point of criminal activity, but oftentimes it is confined to the home and known only to family members. Another person, how-

ever, feeling hooked by a similar conflict will turn the negative emotions toward himself rather than against outside targets. Such a turn creates a different sort of patient, commonly described as depressed. A third person may struggle
against the hooked feeling by fleeing into an unreal world of
dream-like sequences and disconnected behavior which is
commonly called psychosis. On the day I write this news-
papers carried the story of a young man with a history of conflicts and violent emotions who identified himself with John
Lennon and killed the popular musician. Emotionally disturbed people are oftentimes linked with criminals because
both share a feeling of being hooked which oftentimes leads
to forms of violence.

But it is not just criminals and emotionally ill persons who
feel hooked by conflicts and changes in their environment.
We all feel hooked from time to time. We all struggle and do
foolish things and make exaggerated gestures. The serious
cases of emotional disturbance may be statistically rare, but
minor symptoms are known to everyone. No life escapes the
small pains of emotional anguish. In fact, it is well-known to
the physician in family practice that a majority of the symptoms he sees in the clinic come from emotional rather than
physical causes. Not everyone suffers from the worst physical
and emotional illness, but we all become ill from time to time;
and if we do not learn to care for ourselves, we may never get
well. Understanding is the beginning of therapy.

One way of understanding how feelings cause illness is to
elaborate on that simple little metaphor about the trout.
Mental or emotional illness can be made meaningful by seeing it as an inept and ineffective attempt on the part of a person to adjust to environmental upset and upsetting feelings.
Health is a matter of emotional balance, a harmony between
the parts of the self and between the self and the environment. Illness then is an imbalance or a failure of adaptation

which is associated with upsets and conflicts. It is not always the sick person's fault that these disturbances occur. As in the case of the trout, it is frequently some strange element introduced into the life space of a person which causes the upset, the negative feelings, the threatened imbalance, and finally, the bizarre gestures used to relieve it. What we call emotional illness can be understood as inept and expensive gestures to relieve a person who is unable to move about as usual in a harmonious and satisfying way and therefore is overcome with negative feelings.

The gestures a person employs when he feels hooked are worrisome because they are full of aggression. Angry and hateful feelings follow upon a sense of being hooked. Being hooked produces feelings of frustration, anger, and hostility. The odd gestures or crazy behavior of a person come from excessive amounts of anger and fear. Like a dog who is cornered or a fish who is hooked, human beings get scared and angry and show a lot of hostility.

All hostility, of course, is not bad or a sign of illness. Aggressive feelings are natural and provide a needed defense against real threats in the environment. (We do not live in an entirely friendly world.) But once aroused, these feelings often become difficult to control. Sometimes aggression and hostility reach such high levels of intensity that rational discrimination and good judgment go out the window. Children, for example, who are abandoned or mistreated very early in life develop high levels of hostility and aggression which lie around in pools just below the surface of their personality. Later on these feelings leak out in almost everything they do. Their actions, conversations, even their body language express hostility and aggression. The more intense and enduring the aggression, however, the more likely it is to cause emotional illness.

Any number of events can trigger off aggressive and hostile

feelings: a real attack, physical loss, frustration, disappointment, embarrassment, rejection. In effect, then, the environment that is upset can be either internal or external.
Things which simply happen or which people inflict on us
frequently upset our environment. Sometimes, however, the
upset is more the result of the way we understand or misun-
derstand what happens. Either way, a person can feel
hooked, unable to adjust, then angry, hostile, and, finally,
pushed to unusual responses. Negative emotions associated
with a sense of being hooked are the cause of many forms of
illness. Serious physical disease like ankylosing spondylitis
can be caused by these feelings as well as the many common
physical ailments seen most often by the family doctor. And
the same feelings cause what we call emotional illness, both
the serious types treated in mental-health facilities and the
common ones we never bother to get help for.

Emotional disorder or affliction then is a combination of
excess negative emotions and inappropriate devices used to
cope with these feelings. Both together constitute an emotional disorder. If we are going to avoid these problems, we
have to get smarter about our feelings, and about the gestures
or devices we use to manage them. And that we can do and
derive a great benefit from doing it. Each person cannot du-
plicate Norman Cousins' feat, but we can get better control
of our emotions and can become happier and healthier in the
process.

3. Funny things that cause emotional problems

Ordinarily, we assume that the upsets of one's environment
which lead to emotional problems are bad experiences. The
loss of a spouse we know can cause prolonged down feelings,
and people have emotional breakdowns over finanical
disasters. But this is not always the case. Sometimes the emo-

tional upset is brought on by good experiences, happy events or even the realization of a lifelong dream.

A man is finally promoted to a job which he has sought for years and suddenly becomes ill. Now that he has arrived at his new position, there is nothing to struggle for. And besides, there are none of the supports which he had at the lower position. Alone, without a goal, with increased responsibility and fears of failure, he may develop physical ailments or any number of problems which are related to feelings of loss. All of a sudden his environmental situation changes, and he finds it difficult to adjust to new patterns of stress. Like the unfortunate trout, he feels caught, disappointed, down, and, looking ahead, he can see no relief from these depressing feelings.

Similarly it often happens that a girl who dreams of marriage, pursues a handsome boy, captures his affection, plans for and finally has an ideal church wedding, and then, after settling down, begins to develop emotional problems. She, too, suddenly is without a project, and perhaps is a little disappointed in her new husband. Everyone acts as though this should be the happiest time in her life, but she doesn't feel that way at all. Looking ahead she, too, sees only more of the same feelings of disappointment.

Students in college frequently develop emotional problems trying to adjust to the new academic environment. For some, the freedom of college life seems unmanageable; for others the studies create too much stress. Many master their difficulties after an initial period of clumsy performances and go on to finish. Others are never able to find their balance. The new environment seems to be too much for their powers of adjustment. They flop around making inappropriate responses and inadequate gestures, and as exams press closer they feel more and more disturbed. Their options are either to become ill or get away, so most simply leave.

Even one's position in the family can be the cause of emotional upset. A middle child may feel unusual pressure from his family environment. An older brother may have set a standard that he feels unable to meet. He can neither free himself from his family nor from his position in it. He feels frustrated and angry. The same parental demands which helped his older siblings reach their potential and enjoy success come across to him as unfair. Drugs and delinquent behavior may be his ways of coping with these feelings. Such gestures are costly, inept, and they cause great unhappiness. The coping behaviors used by conflicted adolescents (acting out, hypochrondria, passive aggressive behavior) are their ways of handling painful feelings.

The behavior which people often describe as queer or mean or bad can in some cases be looked at as responses to negative feelings. It can be seen as coming from a sense of being hooked, followed by exaggerated gestures to achieve relief. Exaggerated behaviors are unhealthy ways of coping with environmental shifts and conflicts of feelings. And almost any kind of change in life can disturb a person's feelings and lead to the exaggerated and unhealthy devices to cope with these unpleasant emotional states.

A friend of mine has worked all his life in a library cataloging books, mechanically doing the same things over and over again. His routine functions to keep his emotions under control, but when a change occurs in the rigidly controlled environment, he becomes like a caged lion. Even a vacation constitutes a disturbance of his routine and causes problems. The pools of hostility which lie just below the surface cause so many physical ailments that he spends much of his free time and money doctoring. He has never been able to marry, lives alone, and is very unhappy.

Is he just a little odd, or is he so afraid and hostile that unknowingly he adopts these peculiar behaviors as a way of coping? But his adjustment techniques are ineffective (he is always on the edge of blowing up) and contribute to all his physical ills. They also cause alienation from other people, limit his social life, and increase his misery. Why not think of the condition of this man as a form of emotional illness? No physical illness could be any more disruptive of his life.

There are any number of other examples of people who experience life something like the hooked trout. They are overwhelmed with negative feelings and are compelled to make odd gestures or to adopt crazy behaviors in order to relieve these emotional tensions.

Women forced to stay at home alone with children when the husband is called away on a job, for example, often feel trapped, afraid, angry, and adopt all kinds of costly and ineffective devices to regain adjustment or relieve their negative feelings. One woman set fires. Although she denied it adamantly, there was irrefutable proof that she had set fires in the neighborhood and finally burned down her own home. Was she a bad woman? Or was there such a lack of adjustment to her circumstances that she resorted to downright destructive behavior as a relief from built-up bad feelings. The fact that consciously she was unaware of the motives of her behavior increases the similarity of her situation to that of a physical illness.

Then there was the automobile dealer who made a good living but who had to be the most flamboyant spender in the city. He felt that he had to have the flashiest cars, clothes, yacht, house, parties, and to be in the company of celebrities, so he solicited their favor by extravagant gifts. To support this style he stole, and ended up in prison and disgrace. Was he a bad man or was he ill in the sense of using exaggerated gestures to seek relief from fears and emotional conflicts which he did not understand? The relief mechanisms which he adopted, however, only made things worse and ultimately caused his destruction.

Two women live together. They hate men. Their life together is full of angry fights, tears, and jealousies. Are they just queer or are they emotionally disturbed in the sense of suffering from symptoms which are understandable as exaggerated behaviors having their origin in bad feelings or some deep-seated conflict of feelings?

Another woman, educated in the best schools and a member of the social and economic elite, steals little items in homes, stores, offices, and theaters. Is she simply a crook, or is she, too, hooked by some hidden conflict or by some painful feelings which produce these bizarre behaviors?

It is simply not acceptable to say that these men and women are diabolic or that they inherited bad genes. On the other hand, it makes perfectly good sense to inquire about some condition to which they cannot adjust and try to figure out just how their behaviors are analogous to the trout whose crazy flopping around results from feeling out of adjustment with his environment. And it makes sense to look at the bizarre and ineffectual behavior as originating in hostile feelings generated by this sense of being hooked.

Almost any change in one's life causes some stress. When the changes are big ones, or at least are felt to be so, then there is the possiblity of compensating behavior being initiated to relieve fears or feelings of conflict. Some of these compensating behaviors or regulatory devices constitute the symptoms of emotional illness.

4. Who are the doctors for these problems?

The common sense approach to persons engaging in odd and inappropriate behavior is to sit them down and then give them advice about how to straighten out. But this is as useless as calling them bad or blaming everything on genes. If there is an emotional problem at the root of their odd behavior, it cannot simply be advised away. Rather, the real underlying feelings which inappropriate coping devices are being used to hide must be uncovered and exposed. Common sense is a wonderful thing, but following its dictates does not always help people who are emotionally afflicted. If the person who is behaving inappropriately could change just by being given good advice, then most of the big problems in life would be quickly solved. But improving one's feeling states and the strategies used to cope with feelings is usually the end result of many sessions with a trained professional.

Let me give you an example of the differences between a common sense approach and what a professional person would do. On my way to work this morning I heard that a twenty-year-old boy in our little town killed himself in the front yard of his former girlfriend. The two young people had been very close; in fact she had even lived at his parents' home for some time. Then there were arguments and she moved into her own apartment. Finally, she started seeing other boys. After a show-down at a local bar, the boy took a gun and blew out his brains on her front yard.

The news made everyone in town sick. What a waste! What a tragedy! It is easy to imagine the upheaval of emotions brought on by this change in his environment. He really did feel hooked because he could see no way out of his painful emotional situation and made one bizarre gesture to relieve what for him was an unbearable pain. And I'm sure that his friends felt bad because they all would have liked to sit down with him and tell him something like, "She's not worth it," or "You'll forget all about her," or some other bit of common sense.

But none of this would have done any good. He needed someone to listen to him; he needed to hear himself say all the horrible things he wanted to do to her and to himself in order to release his feelings. He needed gradually to understand about bizarre, ineffective, costly and sometimes deadly coping devices from someone who knew just when to talk and how to get over a point. And if none of this had helped in the sense of relieving the overload of bad feelings, then he needed to be hospitalized because at that time he was emotionally ill.

Psychiatrists are the people who, along with psychologists, social workers, brain chemists, and others, make it their business to try to understand hidden conflicts, hostile feelings and the things people do to relieve them. Through the years they have learned a lot about human beings by caring for those whose behavior became so bizarre or dangerous that it required their being withdrawn from the mainstream of life and assigned to the status of patient.

It may seem irreverent to compare people to cars, but if we can be excused for using that analogy, the psychiatrist, like a mechanic, sees only broken-down models. One learns little about engines watching smoothly running vehicles cruise down the highway. Only when they stop functioning normally does someone have to tear them down and find out how they work. Something similar happens with people. Those who break down provide the psychiatrist an opportunity to look deeply into the ways people function and the reasons why their functioning becomes impaired. This information has been collected and organized into theories about how people become emotionally ill, how they get better, and how this form of human distress can be prevented.

One sad aspect of contemporary life is that a great deal of what is known by professionals about common emotional disorders, along with their causes, cures, and prevention, never finds its way to the people who need it. A disturbing change in one's environment is a very common experience, and so too are the feelings of fear and hostility which accompany such a change. But working people cannot afford to see a psychiatrist when they find themselves in some sort of personal crisis. Even if they have the money they may be hesitant to seek professional help for an emotional distress. Unless this information is made available to the greatest possible number of ordinary citizens, a great deal of suffering will continue unnecessarily.

Some psychiatric understanding should be a part of a basic American education. But where is this talked about in the school? Was the young man upset over his girlfriend equipped to get any kind of objective perspective on his tumultuous feelings? Did he know how hostility easily becomes self-punishment and self-destructive? Did he ever hear that life depends upon being able to control the self-destructive consequences of anger and aggressive feelings? Had he ever been convinced that talking over intense feelings is helpful and indeed an absolute necessity in distressing situations? (I wonder whether a continuing case seminar, conducted by a professional, in which different instances of bizarre and destructive behavior were analyzed, would not be more helpful to students than many of the electives they now take like TV Viewing or the History of Football.)

At one time only the rich were able to avail themselves of professional help, and they alone were disposed to seek such help. But things are changing. People in every class and social station get into trouble trying to adjust to life's ups and downs, and professional help in some form is usually available to persons in every socioeconomic group. It can take a number of different forms.

When people think of a professional who treats emotional

upsets, they usually think of the psychiatrist. They are not the only doctors who treat emotional problems, but they are the only ones who are able to write prescriptions for drugs which help relieve very painful feelings. Psychiatrists differ from other mental health professionals in that they have completed a medical degree (M.D.) before spending three or four years in specialized training in emotional illness. Psychiatrists may use any number of different treatment approaches but frequently rely heavily on drugs. They are the experts in body chemistry and especially in the chemistry of the nervous system. Psychiatric training includes study of psychological as well as environmental or social factors in emotional illness, but the primary focus of the training is on the anatomy and physiology of the nervous system. More and more the tendency is for the psychiatrist to stress the biological, physical, or chemical aspects of emotional affliction and to leave the psychological and social concerns to other professionals.

The psychoanalyst may or may not be a physician. If he is, he is a doctor who is the exception to the trend we just referred to. Rather than dispensing medicines and focusing on medical treatment, he or she stresses talk, interpretation, and understanding as the best way of treating emotional distress. There is both short-term and long-term psychoanalytic therapy. The long-term form follows a technique developed by Sigmund Freud and may last five years or more. The typical patient sees the psychoanalyst four times a week for one hour each visit. When you add the number of visits to the length of treatment, it is not difficult to understand why only the rich can avail themselves of classical psychoanalysis.

The short-term treatment is more focused on a specific problem rather than on the whole personality of the patient and can last anywhere from five to fifteen visits. In both long and short-term treatment, the psychiatrist or psychoanalytic therapist uses understanding in the form of anaylsis as the tool for bringing about improvement and change in one's feeling states. Childhood experiences are considered of special importance in the understanding process.

Psychoanalysts are rare outside the large cities, but they have a big influence both on the training of other professionals and even on our popular culture. Words like inferiority complex, introverts, extroverts, repression, identity crisis, and the importance given to sexuality in the media are all examples of the influence of psychoanalysis. The psychoanalysts are looked upon as being the most intellectual of the professionals who work with emotional disorders.

Another doctor one may find in a hospital or a neighborhood clinic has a Ph.D. rather than an M.D. degree. He or she is a psychologist rather than a psychiatrist. The training of the psychologist may be involved with both human beings and animals and may cover different ways of explaining behavior. Where the psychiatrist looks at emotional upsets from the perspective of medical science, the psychologist's viewpoint is formed by nonmedical theorists such as Skinner, Piaget, existentialist philosophers, and others. Personality theory and development of personality are thoroughly studied by psychologists. In working with emotionally disturbed people, the psychologist may conduct therapy sessions or may focus on diagnostic testing. Many of the sophisticated testing instruments for understanding patients were developed by research psychologists, and practicing or clinical psychologists usually administer and interpret these tests. In a hospital setting both psychologists and psychiatrists are found on the staff.

If the psychiatrist emphasizes the biological aspect of emotional illness, and the psychologist the psychological aspects of it, the social worker emphasizes the role of family in emotional disturbance. In a mental-health unit, the psychiatrist would manage the medication, the psychologist would do the testing and the social worker would get the family history and try to help the patient by working for changes in family relationships. Social workers do therapy with patients, but it either includes the family or is carried on in groups. The education of the social worker may have reached the master's rather than the doctoral level, but the master in social work degree is a difficult and demanding accomplishment. It involves much the same kind of theory mastering and work with patients which is required of the psychiatrist and psychologist.

Psychiatrists, psychologists, social workers, because of long years of study and daily contact with patients, know a lot about emotional upsets, adjustment problems, and exaggerated devices to control or relieve feelings. What has been learned by these professional persons in treating desperate, deluded, and disorgainzed people with angry and hostile feelings needs to be given broader dissemination. This information, as the case of the young boy in our little town illustrates, may literally be a matter of life and death.

5. *Interesting facts about emotions*

Can anything about the emotions be factual? Don't we use the word *fact* to refer to something which stands out so that it can be recognized by everyone? Emotional, however, refers to a very private rather than a public experience. In fact, emotional seems to be just the opposite of factual. What we feel or think is recognizable by others only through the use of signs and symbols.

And yet we can talk about the facts of emotional life in the sense of certain very common human experiences. Certain inner experiences, like things in the outside world, can be verified over and over again. Describe for me your fear, anger, hate, jealousy, sexual desire, anxiety, aggression, and I will recognize the experience as ones which I, too, have had.

It is also a "fact" that frightful and traumatic experiences, especially when they occur in childhood, tend to be pushed out of consciousness in order to relieve the associated psychic pain. One way to handle something painful or frightening is simply to forget it. We human beings can repress both feelings and events so that painful aspects of life are not remembered. Not only is repression a fact in the sense of a commonplace, but it is also a fact that the repressed memories continue to influence later experience even though we are not consciously aware of what is happening.

When a conflict with all its frightening and frustrating feelings is repressed, it causes all kinds of disturbance. Inadequate mothering, for example, can create a conflict between loving and hating the same person. In order to avoid the conflict and its pain, the hateful feelings may simply be repressed or forgotten. Later on, however, these emotions reemerge in physical symptoms like headaches, gastro-intestinal pain, asthma, and sexual impotence. In other cases repressed conflicts and their accompanying negative feelings find an outlet in immoral or criminal behaviors like promiscuity, delinquency, and shoplifting. Human behaviors that resemble the gestures of a hooked fish are ways of relieving painful inner feelings, and this is so even when the feeling of being hooked is the result of conflicts and pain which are forgotten or repressed.

The case of a woman called Anna O. had a great influence on Sigmund Freud and illustrates just how frightening experiences are pushed out of consciousness only to cause disturbances of both a physical and an emotional sort. Anna was an intelligent and attractive woman, twenty-one years old, who developed many ailments in connection with the illness and death of her father. On the physical side, she developed paralysis in her limbs, parts of her body went numb, she had a nervous cough, and lost interest in eating. She changed back and forth between two different personalities; one her normal self, and the other a trance-like indifferent personality. All this happened in connection with a very frightening change in her life situation and accompanying negative feelings.

Anna was very close to her father and very fond of him. His sickness and death created in her such anger and fright that she did not feel able to manage it. Her way of coping was to push all the frightening thoughts and feelings out of consciousness. She kept her balance by simply forgetting what had happened. But like all unhealthy coping devices, this was not a real solution. The events surrounding her father's last illness had stirred up intensely painful emotions. Her own developing sexual maturity and the question of what to do with her life increased her emotional fright. The new environment she was forced to face was too much for her to handle without her father. She didn't know how to cope. She could not imagine how such a thing could happen to her or what would become of her. Instead of adjusting to what was happening, she used the technique of putting it all out of her mind. She couldn't remember things about her father's death or anything at all about his last days.

But the emotions associated with these memories did not go away. The fright and fear, anger and hostility came out in all her physical and emotional symptoms. When she was able to think through the painful events and face up to the many negative feelings which were associated with them, then her symptoms disappeared.

In Anna's case, like many others, emotional illness originated in an inability to adjust to painful changes taking place in life, followed by the adoption of coping devices for her feelings which in the long run turn out to be costly, painful, and ineffective. And her illness was cured not by telling her things like, "This is all in your head," or "This does not make good sense," but by helping her to remember the painful events, to talk through her feelings, and thereby to adjust to what had happened. Just knowing about Anna and how her emotional illness developed may help some persons to handle a difficult situation better. Understanding by itself creates alternatives to the expensive but unproductive gestures that are part of every emotional affliction.

Would you believe that dreams by night and fantasies by day are also connected to the same repressed memories and feelings which generate the expensive and unproductive gestures which are called the symptoms of emotional illness? Just as bad coping devices can be traced back to changes in life which cause a person to feel hooked and angry and afraid, the same can be said for dreams and daytime fantasies. Yes, even these seemingly meaningless psychic activities become intelligible when connected to predominant feelings and frightening events of a personal life history. The most bizarre dream images can be connected to bits and pieces of the previous day's events, and we can make some superficial sense of them by so doing. But the deeper meanings are derived from looking at the dream images as ways of relieving, during sleep, the unresolved emotional problems of our past. Psychiatrists want to hear about our dreams because it is "a fact" that dreams give important clues about the forgotten experiences that continue to influence a life. Time and time again it has been found that in discussing a dream, persons can be led to discover material from the past which they were unable to deal with at the time and, therefore, repressed. Usually, but not always, this involves very early childhood experience.

One student in a class I teach on "Sleep and Dreams" had a history of very disruptive sleep disturbances which made it difficult for her to keep a roommate. Whenever there were changes in her life which created stress like exams or an upset relationship, she would sit up periodically during the night and scream. Although she remembered nothing about these incidents the next morning, her night terrors kept everyone within hearing distance awake and frightened.

After listening to her description of the scenes which were associated with her fits of screaming, a common thread emerged. Although the scenes were different, they all involved something falling on her or threatening to cover her up. As she talked about the frightening feelings and scenes, she began to remember, if only dimly at first, an event in her childhood which was particularly frightening and involved a mirror in the hall at home falling on her. She went home and talked to her mother who helped her remember two separate incidents involving objects falling on people. Once her mother was caught under a heavy object which fell from the wall, and on another occasion a heavy mirror fell on the girl when she pulled out a drawer of the dresser to which the mirror was attached.

Just as in physical illness, the emotionally afflicted person loses contact with the underlying cause of the distress. People do not know what caused them to become ill. In emotional illness the feelings which are at the root of the problem as well as the original upsetting event are lost from memory. Because the cause is unknown, the remedy for the problem also escapes us. No wonder this situation is referred to as an illness. The surprising thing about this type of illness is that it can be relieved by bringing the forgotten incident and feelings to consciousness. Just understanding what is going on or how certain coping devices function in our lives is often enough to start the healing process.

While at home and now much older and more mature, my student was able to go over the events, see where they had happened, understand how they had happened and see that there was no longer a reason to be afraid. Getting in touch with the memory and understanding it as an adult was all that was needed. The buried negative feelings which had endured for years and were stirred up whenever something upsetting occurred, underwent an immediate modification. The bizarre sleep behaviors which were used to cope with her repressed fears were no longer necessary, and the night terrors stopped. Years of painfully disruptive and ineffective behavior ended when the underlying feeling and events were better understood and integrated into a more mature personality.

Whenever this student felt hooked or tense, or frightened by something happening in her life, the associated feelings tapped into a pool of similar frightful emotions which remained with her from early childhood. Her way of coping was to relieve fearful events in a childlike attempt to master the emotions during sleep. The result was a coping device which also qualified as a sleep symptom or a sleep disorder. The night terrors did provide an outlet for her negative emotions, but it was a costly way of managing them. This strategy disrupted her life and the lives of everyone around her. And there were better ways of managing. Once she understood what was happening, where the feelings came from, and how they were triggered by the current conflicts or trauma, the costly coping devices were replaced by more effective and healthier ways.

It is a fact that every life has its buried and forgotten traumatic elements. When these are very intense and are associated with intense feelings of fear, anger and aggression, they force us to employ coping devices or ways of keeping our balance in the face of forces which could cause us to collapse. The balancing gestures or regulating devices can be just mildly dysfunctional like night terror attacks or phobias, but they can also be so severe as to require hospitalization. Even the bizarre behaviors which we associate with severe mental breakdowns are understandable as coping devices. So are the personality disorders we will turn to next. In a sense they help the afflicted person to cope but they do so at too high a price.

These "facts" a psychiatrist meets time and time again in clinical practice. All this and more could be cited as evidence that there is a factual dimension even to subtle inward personal experience. These "facts" may be differently understood and differently treated, but they appear in varieties of persons in all ages and in different cultures. Our goal in this book is to organize these facts into clusters or units so as to help people recognize them in themselves and thereby understand themselves a little better when they feel hooked or act crazy. Understanding is not everything but it is ninety percent of the struggle to find relief and a modest amount of satisfaction in life.

6. *Understanding unusual behavior*

The behaviors of human beings are like a text written in a foreign language. One must develop a key in order to translate them into something which can more easily be understood. A theory of personality is just such a key. My goal is to present a viewpoint that anyone can understand and use to make sense out of his own life.

Freud focused on man's drive for sensual satisfaction and made sense out of bizarre behavior by linking it to this impulse. Freud was able to relieve many of the painful symptoms developed by his patients by exposing the underlying and forgotten sexual conflict which caused them to occur. While not ignoring sexual feelings, the focus in this perspective is on the aggressive ones. We will be trying to understand the meaning of a bizarre behavior by connecting it to aggressive and hostile feelings. Our code or key translation device focuses on the negative emotions. The odd behaviors of the emotionally disturbed are made understandable by linking them up to underlying angry and destructive feelings.

Take criminal behavior as an example. Karl Menninger has crusaded all his life to have the penal system become more responsive to persons in prisons because he sees many, but not all, as emotionally disturbed and not simply bad. Certain criminals repeat their unlawful actions over and over again, trying to satisfy an urge to hurt. Merely locking these people up and punishing them is comparable to locking up and punishing people suffering from a chronic infection.

Some criminals are dominated by an unconscious impulse to hurt the environment. Others are trying to hurt themselves. And this is true of more than just criminals. Many other forms of emotional affliction are symbolic self-hurting—a way of punishing oneself for some offense or for failing to live up to some expectation. In fact, the most common forms of emotional problems referred for professional help, like depression, alcoholism, hypochondria, are outright forms of self-punishment. Suicide is the ultimate or most intense expression of this type of illness.

When faced with a puzzling change in someone's behavior, then, we can begin to try to understand by asking: What is this odd and unusual behavior doing for the person? What function is it performing? We all have difficulty keeping our emotions in balance. When we get out of adjustment with our environment we talk about being under stress, and we complain about feeling tense. Stress and tension can reach the point where they threaten to overwhelm us, and then emergency coping devices are deployed. The trout's odd behaviors are gestures adopted in order to cope with a disturbance in his ordinary adjustment with the environment. Similarly certain human behaviors may seem strange and senseless to the casual observer, but they too can be made meaningful by seeing them as attempts to manage unusual stress or to cope with excessive tension. Craziness then is a management device. Anything is preferable to falling apart or going to pieces emotionally.

Because stress and tension activate aggressive feelings, hostility and a wish to hurt are always part of the picture. The hooked trout is angry and frustrated, and his crazy behaviors are a form of striking out. Aggressive striking out is not usually well thought out, and therefore it tends to be ineffective.

Costly, ineffective, unproductive releases of hostility while under great stress—this is one way of understanding emotional illness. While the intention of a person may be to keep his balance or to manage the tension, the emergency devices employed miss the mark. They are more hurtful than helpful. In the short run, they may work. An alcoholic, for example, relieves his tension with a drink; a junkie does the same thing with some other drug; an adolescent feels a sense or relief vandalizing the school; and the anorexic girl feels safe as long as she does not eat. But in the long run these management devices are mainly hurtful. They are maintained at an increasingly costly price. Actually, what they do is cause more pain. They add to the negative feelings and in the process constitute the symptoms of emotional affliction.

Emotional illness then is not like physical illness. It has little to do with viruses and bacteria. There are cases in which something physical or chemical goes wrong which produces crazy behavior. If this happens, getting better is simply a matter of finding the right pill to restore the proper physical or chemical balance. But in other cases there are no pills which help. The illness, unlike cellular abnormality, is a set of unusual reactions to cope with overwhelming negative feelings.

Seeing emotional problems simply as an imbalance in brain chemistry is very much in vogue today, and taking this perspective can stimulate development of newer and better psychiatric drugs. But drugs and chemistry are not now and never will be the whole answer. Besides body chemistry, emotional problems involve dispositions, attitudes, distorted meanings, ideas, motives, a social environment with which the person must find an adequate adjustment, and finally, they involve a cluster of negative feeling states.

Emotional affliction, according to this perspective, is a term used for persons who are obliged to make awkward and expensive maneuvers to maintain their balance or to avoid falling apart emotionally.

An emotional affliction is a faulty technique for keeping one's balance under the pressure of threatening negative feelings. It is a survival technique for a particularly stressful time.

A person with an emotional problem adopts behavior that is designed to cope with painful negative feelings but which causes suffering to the self, isolation from one's fellows, harassment and social disgrace. And yet for the person overwhelmed with negative feelings, it seems the thing to do in order to find relief and to keep from falling apart emotionally.

The basic idea behind this explanation of behavior was set out in very plain English by a novelist at the turn of this century:

> All our lives long, every day and every hour, we are en-gaged in the process of accommodating our changed and unchanged selves to changed and unchanged surroundings; living, in fact, is nothing else than this process of accom-modation; when we fail in it a little we are stupid, when we fail flagrantly we are mad, when we suspend it temporarily we sleep, when we give up the attempt altogether we die. In quiet, uneventful lives the changes internal and external are so small that there is little or no strain in the process of fusion and accommodation; in other lives there is great strain, but there is also great fusing and accommodating power; in others great strain with little accommodating power. A life will be successful or not, according as the power of accommodation is equal to or unequal to the strain of fusing and adjusting internal and external changes.[2]

The key words are accommodation and interaction. The key is that human life is in constant dynamic interaction with an environment, other persons, organizations, facts, drives, impulses, and needs. This means that life is full of contingen-cies. The unexpected is always happening. Emergencies are commonplace, and they push feelings into the negative range. There are the misbehaviors of other persons, and the occur-rences of disruptive events. The inevitabilities of birth and death generate strong emotions and are difficult to manage. Growth creates a special sort of stress. Providing personal satisfaction and security for others means postponing these feelings in oneself and puts strain even on mature persons.

Becoming emotionally ill in the sense of developing what

the textbooks call neuroses, personality disorders, or even psychoses, is the outward evidence of a struggle going on within the person to adapt or to accommodate to threatening and painful feelings. To be emotionally afflicted is not to have a germ or a virus, but rather to have adopted a set of adaptive measures for handling bad feelings that are not wholly effective. These ineffective measures have their own structure and appear with little variation from age to age, culture to culture. As such they lend themselves to labels which provide shorthand symbols or easy ways to talk about these measures.

Emotional illness is not the same as physical illness but the two are comparable. When the body develops fever, swelling, redness, pain, it is trying to adjust to antibodies which threaten normal body balance. The physician understands these coping devices and tries to work with them to bring the patient back to his prior healthy state. In a similar way, the psychiatrist sees the behavioral oddities of emotional affliction as attempts to reestablish emotional balance. The first task of the professional helper is to understand the function of these symptoms by interpreting them and suggesting alternatives to guide the person back to a more normal state where effective rather than ineffective adaptive measures are used.

Each new situation creates a new challenge to the task of adjustment and requires renewed efforts to keep one's feelings within the positive range. Menninger liked to compare life to paddling a canoe in a fast-flowing stream. There are periods of relative calm and then there are times when all manner of skill and effort are required just to keep from going under. An individual person's best efforts on occasion may not be enough. The current can catch him in an awkward position and throw him out of the boat. Or the canoe can get hung up and spring a leak. These are emergency situations which require emergency tactics and possibly outside help. Complicating things even more, some persons have distinct vulnerability (their boat is weak or has an easily bruised skin; they have no swimming ability or weak paddling skills.). For them the emergency situation may be so serious that it requires discontinuing the trip. They literally have to get out of the water and spend some time being laid up. Here a psychiatrist comes to the aid by assigning to such a person the status of patient, which includes a societal justification for withdrawing from ordinary responsibilities.

Another person may not be quite so vulnerable. He may have to flounder around a little, perhaps send up some distress signals (symptoms) so that someone on shore may be alerted and give a hand. That hand, in the sense of a bit of help, may be all he needs. Although still a little shaky and feeling more nervous and anxious than usual, he is nevertheless able to get back on course. One little bit of emergency help was all that was needed. But we can also imagine the help going on for quite some time before the person is able to snap back.

Then too, some people are always in trouble. They constantly signal for help. (They are the ones we have to hide from on occasion.) Others pretty well manage their own problems. Their work, their organized patterns, their close family ties, their friends, all combine to provide the shock absorbers for inevitable bumps. Rarely do they show signs of emotional disequilibrium. They manage to come up with the extra efforts on occasion to keep feelings balanced, to avert a threat, to achieve a goal, to handle a loss. Like rich men they always seem to be able to pay the price for maintaining equilibrium. But if there are a few rich, there are many poor.

Psychiatrists have learned a lot about emotional problems from years of working with poor and unfortunate people.

What they learned may not qualify as facts in any strict scientific sense, but it comes close. Like other lessons provided by experience, psychiatric understanding is verified time and again in practice.

We mentioned above how frightful and traumatic events, like the death of Anna O.'s father, throw a person off balance and if managed by repression or forgetting can produce psychiatric symptoms. The fact is that frightening events in early childhood affect every life. But it is also true that single upsetting events seldom have as much effect as continued painful or frustrating relationships between child and parent. Children are affected by the death of a parent, but such a single occurrence seldom seals a child's psychic fate. Children may have trouble grieving, but they can grieve and can come through a mourning process in good emotional health. It is the prolonged unsatisfactory relationship with sick, alcoholic, or inadequate parents that tends to do the most harm. These keep the child continually off balance. It is a "fact" that in such cases, fear, hostility, and aggression build up and what we call the symptoms of mental illness develop as efforts to adjust or accommodate.

Environmental changes cause emotional upset which then may lead to the adoption of crippling accommodating behaviors which constitute emotional illness, or lead to the adoption of effective adjustment behaviors which constitute emotional health. The difference between health and illness hinges on the behaviors or coping devices which are adopted for feeling states. Costly and ineffective coping devices not only constitute the symptoms of emotional illness, but increase the negative feelings which lie behind them. Anxiety and aggression increase with the use of these bad accommodating mechanisms, and consequently so does unhappiness.

Certain coping devices are associated with minor degrees of emotional upset, others are linked with more serious problems, and still others are characteristic of good adjustment or happiness. One of the important lessons a layman can learn from the professional psychiatrist is to recognize coping devices for what they are, and learn to differentiate the healthier ones from those which are unhealthy. Just recognizing these differences for what they are makes it possible to understand an emotionally afflicted person and perhaps even to love him.

Martin Luther King, for example, seemed to have an understanding of white people who were overwhelmed with anger and hatred. He understood that bigotry was a way of managing fear and guilt and self-hatred. Without such an understanding, he would have responded to hate with more hate. Understanding something about destructive human feelings and the devices people use to cope with these feelings made it possible for him to move beyond racial hatred to reconciliation. He tried to help both the white and the black man. Dr. King's life shows the strength and power which can come from understanding.

We can understand a lot about costly and ineffective coping strategies by looking at racial or religious bigotry. The bigot uses a coping mechanism called projection. Feelings of fear and hostility threaten to overcome a personality plagued by low self-esteem and insecurity. In order to keep balance, these personal fears and hostilities (usually unacknowledged) are projected into others or unloaded onto them. This makes the other—black, Jew, Catholic—someone to fear and hate. Instead of trying to handle one's own negative feelings, all efforts are directed at defeating the hated other. The use of this coping device explains prejudice, bigoted behavior, and hypervigilance. It can contribute to eccentric and abrasive personality styles. In its worst forms it constitutes paranoia and really serious emotional illness.

Another coping device associated with serious affliction is denial. The person who uses repression does not know about his frightening or threatening feeling states ("I don't feel anything," or "I am not angry"). Denial, however, operates on external reality. People who do not exist are brought into being. Others who do exist are changed to become someone else ("I am Jesus Christ," "He is the devil"). Denial manages threatening feelings by changing outside reality into something less threatening.

Other ways of altering or managing upsetting feelings and threatening situations are more common. They are used from time to time even by generally healthy people. During a time of crisis they may be employed by a basically healthy person but not held onto. Less healthy people tend to get stuck in their use and by so doing come across to others as having quirks or hangups. Here we are referring to accommodating devices which are characteristic of the less serious forms of emotional problems.

Intellectualization, for example, is a way of handling upsetting feelings by thinking or talking about them, but only in a bland and formalized way. A professor may use such a technique. He may for example pay a great deal of attention to the literature about death, theories of death, the psychology and sociology of dying people. All the formal and theoretical talk may be a way of avoiding the threatening feelings he himself has about dying. Busy work, excessive ritual, and other such coping devices are closely associated with intellectualization.

Displacement is another common coping device. It involves the substitution of things, strangers, or animals for important other persons about whom we have intense feelings. The man who manages his anger at his boss by kicking the dog is using this accommodation strategy. So is the fellow who smashes the door instead of his wife. People who tell hostile ethnic jokes may be using it as well. Most phobias, too, are examples of this redirection of feelings to another object which is less threatening.

Reaction formation is an interesting adjustment device which shows the symbol-making capacity of human beings. It involves adopting a behavior diametrically opposed to threatening or immoral feelings. A woman for example who feels attracted to someone else's husband may treat him like a piece of dirt. Conversely she may treat someone she intensely dislikes with formalized deference and attention.

We'll see more about these not-so-healthy accommodation mechanisms when we look at the different levels of seriousness in emotional affliction. At this point it is sufficient to suggest that understanding these different coping devices for what they are can help us to understand the meaning of becoming emotionally ill as well as the meaning of getting well. The categories of coping devices along with their labels provide some insight into hidden emotions and some rationality to what seems on the surface to be nothing but stupid behavior. Understanding what the different coping mechanisms are, and what causes them to be employed, takes us a long way along the road of understanding ourselves as well as other persons. But no one goes to the end of the road; we never completely understand.

We can rejoice in what we know but must be aware of the limitations of our knowledge. Why does one person adopt this coping device for negative feelings and another person in the same family adopt a different one? When did the adoption of a particular coping strategy occur? How did it happen? The origin of coping devices, like the origins of the feelings they manage, is clouded in mystery. There is always an upset of some sort, an inner conflict, a sense of being hooked, hostile and aggressive feelings, but these interact with biological disposition, early family relations, and childhood experiences. A bit of help at a crucial time can turn a person away from ineffective adjustments and toward a healthy set of coping devices. Identification with an uncle or a baseball star or a homosexual teacher may also turn a person in one or another direction. Genes play a part, so does biochemistry. All these factors mix with many others in creating the emotionally disturbed or emotionally healthy person.

Getting better, however, is much easier to understand than becoming ill. A turn toward health in a hospitalized patient occurs when he or she stops blaming other people and starts accepting responsibility for feelings and events. Improvement is also obvious when the formerly disturbed person begins to employ the coping devices which are characteristic of healthy and well-adjusted people.

If there are certain devices or behaviors that constitute illness, there are others which constitute health. These healthy techniques integrate outside reality with private feelings and promote personal relationships. To the layman they may appear as moral virtues. Charity, caring for others, thoughtfulness, and altruism are examples both of virtues and of healthy coping devices. They are healthy not only because they facilitate adjustment but because they provide satisfaction and promote positive feelings.

Playing and humor are also healthy strategies. They reflect both good adjustment and positive emotions and help bring about both. Humor, for example, permits us to face the unpleasant aspects of life by substituting positive for negative feelings. Both humor and laughing help us to bear up with painful experience and, like the virtues, provide satisfaction in doing so. The healthy benefits of games and exercise are obvious.

Other examples of healthy coping devices and signs of good emotional adjustment include suppression, in the sense of an ability to postpone certain feelings for a time. This technique makes it possible to minimize discomfort, use a stiff upper lip, to postpone attention to trouble and problems and feelings until they can be most effectively resolved. Suppression makes it possible to postpone action on painful feelings or disturbing situations, whereas repression puts both out of consciousness.

Anticipation is another healthy coping device and sign of good emotional health. It involves a capacity to plan for the future and to prepare for discomfort that is on the horizon. Unhealthy people are always surprised by disruptions and frustrations; healthy people on the other hand not only realistically expect painful feelings and conflicts that go with life, but try to prepare ahead even for death.

Sublimation is a term used to describe the very healthy capacity to channel unstructured energies into creative and constructive activities. The artist is a classic example of someone who turns oftentimes negative and destructive feelings into something beautiful. Through sublimation feelings are modified so that other persons are benefited from their expression, and in the process the artist gains satisfaction as well. The biographies of great artists, musicians, and poets are full of instances in which, through sublimation, potentially destructive emotions were redirected to the creation of something beautiful.

Other examples of ordinary coping devices which fall within the healthy range include: touching, making love, listening to good music, eating a satisfying meal, smoking an occasional pipe, chewing gum or tobacco, having a drink, laughing, crying, exercising self-discipline, sleeping, dreaming, working, and talking about feelings.

7. *Personalities twisted by threatening feelings*

People are more complicated than what can be portrayed by identifying coping devices and listing strategies. By a process that defies our ability to understand completely each person pulls together inherited physical and mental capacities into a unified self which we talk about as character or personality. Some personality units are able to adapt to changing stressful situations. Others are inflexible and afraid to change. When weak personality structures come under extraordinary stress they become vulnerable to the serious forms of emotional disturbance.

The term personality includes the physical and emotional aspects of the person: his loves and hates, disposition, willpower, hopes; what he had been and what he aims at becoming. Certain aspects of this complex unity we simply find ourselves with, such as a nervous or a placid disposition, a tendency to worry or not to worry, high or low intelligence, a sense of humor, sensitivity, or its absence. Other aspects we create by a strong will, intense commitment, and by the influence of powerful ideals. What we are as children of particular parents does not finally determine our personality, but it does set some kind of limit on just what we will be able to make of ourselves. Although those features which we find ourselves with cannot be removed, they can be modified. Personality is as much a matter of freedom, and a testimony to continued effort, as it is a reflection of fate or talent. Personality is like a work of art.

It is this undetermined aspect of ourselves, the idea of personality as possibility rather than fate, that makes the efforts of parents and teachers and pastors so needed and so worthwhile. It is this openness to many different futures which makes parents, friends, and helpful people so important in the formation of a human personality. A good influence at a crucial time in a person's life can literally change the course of his or her personality development. And finally it is this same openness which explains incidences of emotional affliction and even personality collapse under the pressure of threatening feelings and events.

Returning to the trout metaphor, it is not a coping device which has to adjust to the disturbed environment, but a personality. In the continuing give-and-take between the person and his situation, some personalities are in the habit of failing, while others always seem to be able to adjust. We all start out as helpless babies, and we remain somewhat vulnerable throughout life. There were times when our development could have gone differently with a change of luck or the influence of different significant persons. But where there is life, there is always the possibility of change and healthier modifications. Personality can mature and it can regress. People improve their personalities, and in some cases personalities become worse. In some cases deterioration reaches the point of constituting an emotional disorder.

We all have some idea of what is meant by a personality breakdown, but to get an idea of a personality disorder that is less severe and much more common let's look at a personality which seems drawn to the abuse of alcohol. Not every alcoholic suffers from a personality disorder, but frequently a deep-seated and built-in personality weakness underlies alcoholic behavior. Characteristic of personality disorders generally, the alcoholic may find no problem with his behavior. Those around him who suffer from his style of life are usually more pained and hurt by his behavior that he is. They can see certain personality traits linked with his alcohol abuse, but these connections are hard for him to make. The person suffering from a phobia knows that his fears are unreasonable and feels that the phobic behavior is alien to his real, deeper, or better self. In some alcoholics, however, there is no sense of anything being wrong. The unhealthy coping devices are so integrated into the self that they become one with the personality rather than being sensed as alien to one's better self.

Among alcoholics one finds a surprising number of personalities which in common language are simply referred to as "spoiled." The term "spoiled" suggests that the person was given too much or was babied too long, thereby contributing to the development later in life of a personality which is unable to manage deprivation. Reality, both social and natural, makes demands on adults which come over to the spoiled person as unjust and send him in search of relief.

If the child is showered with constant gifts by parents, he or she may come to expect other people to continue this practice. Oversolicitous or overprotective parents may contribute to a personality characterized by unrealistic expectations. Unrealistic expectations in their turn set up the conditions for constant disappointment with all its accompanying anger, aggression, and hostility. Drinking then may become a way of anesthetizing these negative feelings. Alcohol abuse for the spoiled personality can be a way of expressing feelings of revenge for all the disappointments of life, and at the same time be a means of gaining satisfaction, as children do, by putting something into the mouth. One can never receive too much love, but too much of some of the material dimensions of loving can have very negative influences in personality development.

A youngest child may be babied, over-protected, and kept in a childlike relationship to parents for too long. (Some spoiling almost inevitably goes on with the last child.) But even the last child must grow up. His or her privileged position with the parents ultimately must be relinquished. The crucial question is whether such a child will be able to manage the transition to adult life. Will more gratification or protection be expected than adult life can provide? Will a demanding personality develop which is rarely ever satisfied? If so, the resulting disappointment and frustration can lead to the use of alcohol as a management device for what has become a deep-seated personality structure.

Besides making the drinker feel good, warm, and comforted, alcohol abuse can at the same time express feelings of hostility and even revenge against whatever factors cause frustration. For the spoiled, infantile, or oral personality, drinking can be a way of repeating early infantile experience, when warm feelings of satisfaction centered around the mouth. At the same time it can cause pain indirectly to parents, spouse, or other persons who are alternately loved and hated as a small child alternately loves and hates his parents.

Disappointments or frustrations can leave a spoiled personality embittered, and alcohol then can become a childish way of managing the associated negative feelings. Mature ways of handling such feelings, characteristic of a more mature personality, include expressing complaints in a proper setting thereby getting them "off the chest," or sublimating disappointment by turning the energy generated into more productive activity. But these mature traits require a strength which is beyond imagining for a childish or spoiled personality.

Another factor frequently found in an alcoholic personality is exaggerated insecurity. Feelings of insecurity may be as hidden to the alcoholic as is the function of alcohol in compensating for them. My favorite alcoholic, one with whom I have spent a great deal of time, is a classic example of this particular personality type. Every time he gets drunk it is like turning on a record entitled, "Look at what a great guy I am." It doesn't take a Sigmund Freud to catch a glimpse of his deep-seated underlying insecurity.

But in many cases the feelings of insecurity and inferiority are much more subtle. They depend very little upon a realistic analysis of the person's actual situation and very much upon long-forgotten childhood experiences. As a child, the alcoholic may have endured a bitter disappointment. Or he may have felt betrayed or unloved, or unfairly treated. These early experiences may be completely forgotten. Although they are no longer conscious, they contributed to a personality development and now influence an adult lifestyle. The feelings which were engendered—feelings of frustration, guilt, insecurity, fear, possibly even rage—continue to operate unconsciously. These early events and the associated feelings may dominate the alcoholic's personality.

It is interesting that the earlier the emotional experience occurs, the greater the chance of causing such a psychic wound that one part of the psyche does not move with the rest through normal stages of development. An otherwise mature personality may retain in one area a strong similarity to the small child he was when a certain trauma occurred, and like that child he tries to achieve satisfaction and relief orally. Personality formation is always something of a mystery. This is as true of the so-called normal personalites as it is for the persons with painful personality disorders.

Unconscious feelings of insecurity or resentment, and even a degree of rage, are part of every personality structure. Every child meets with frustration and disappointment. We all have to move from a stage where everything is pleasure and satisfaction to the stage where we have to confront that rough real world with its displeasures and dissatisfactions.

Every child is weaned and experiences feelings of rage at the deprivation. Separation from momma leaves a mark on all us boys. And who did not suffer a disappointment when he had to give up believing in Santa Claus? So, in a sense, we are all potential alcoholics. The actual alcoholic may have had these common traumas and other uncommon ones to manage. Or he may have been a little weaker when the common frustration and unpleasant feelings came along.

We tend not to notice or not to pay much attention to successful adjustments between personality and the inevitable stresses of life. Some men and women seem to manage their homes and children without attracting much attention. There are, for example, career persons who move up the hierarchical ladder in smooth and measured steps. Successful adjustments of personality to environment are less conspicuous than unsuccessful ones.

It is when personalities fail to adjust and instead adopt bizarre gestures to handle their discomfort that we are forced to take notice. Failure may follow from a particularly difficult set of environmental stresses like loss of a job, or death of a spouse, with all the accompanying negative feelings. Or it sometimes happens that what we would describe as an ordinary upset turns out to be too much for one personality to handle. Criticism at work, for example, can throw some persons into a tailspin. A conflict with spouse or child or a case of winter flu may be all that is required to cause another to go into collapse. Ordinarily, however, severe personality disorders follow upon painful emotional experiences early in life which undermine normal development.

Anorexia nervosa is an example of just such a severe disorder. Anorexia is a Greek word which means loss of appetite but in psychiatric language it refers to an unusual form of personality illness which generally afflicts young women. If there is one personality problem which obviously comes across as an illness and at the same time is characteristic of our culture, it is anorexia. Like the alcoholic, the anorexic is dominated by feelings of fear, but she is afraid to put anything into her mouth. Protesting all along that she is too fat, the anorexic starves herself into a skeletal frailty and in some cases starves herself to death.

In Freud's time there were many hysterical personalities, women who tried to maintain their balance in a strict puritanical culture with personality traits characterized by repression of forbidden sexual feelings. Now it is the anorexic personality that is common enough today to become a characteristic problem of our age. The affected person looks sick, and unless something is done, death may result. Anorexia is a serious mental illness which has its roots in strong negative emotions and is closely bound to the personality of the sufferer.

If the nineteenth-century hysteric reflected cultural expectations of women then, the anorexic does the same for our century. The anorexic is most frequently a shy, controlled, perhaps naive female, and like her nineteenth-century sister she retreats into illness because of demands being made on her. Now, however, it is the demand to perform rather than to restrain that causes psychic stress. Rather than the limited options of a puritanical culture, it is the unlimited options of our liberated age that cause feelings of terror and contribute to the development of a personality which retreats into symptoms. Because of the preoccupation of our culture with thinness, it is not surprising the symptoms of anorexia include exaggerated thinness and obsessiveness about food.

Statistics on anorexia are hard to gather, but some put the figure at one case in every 200 middle-class families. Descriptions of the disorder have not changed much over the years.

An adolescent girl from a close-knit family, who has either been a fussy eater herself or associated with a mother preoccupied with eating and weight, goes on a diet and after a few months has everyone alarmed with her skeletal appearance. Neither persuasion nor threats can shake her out of her abstinence. In fact, the stronger the protests, the more obstinate she becomes. Typical of other personality disorders, the anorexic does not experience her behavior as symptomatic. It is others who are alarmed and see her behavior as unbalanced and disordered.

Gradually everything centers around weight and food. Her ideas about herself as fat or in danger of getting fat become delusional. Laxatives are abused, and oftentimes vomiting is induced to rid the body of dreaded food. Although her preoccupation with her body is hypochondriacal, rather than complain of illness, she claims that she never felt better or that her skeletal appearance is in fact her best weight. Underneath the pathetic physical appearance is a personality which is terrorized by the body and the horror of the fleshly developments associated with womanhood. Denial plays a prominent role in this personality disorder. The anorexic adamantly denies that she is either ill or thin or hungry. In other forms of emotional illness the problematic behavior is recognized as alien to the real self, but in anorexia, characteristic of personality disorders generally, there is no such recognition, Naturally this makes therapy much more difficult.

For the anorexic, the body is the enemy and must be brought under the strictest control if the personality is to survive. Self-starvation paradoxically becomes a life project and is pursued with feverish dedication. The young girl overwhelmed by feelings of fear sets out to create a new personality and to gain both respect and attention by following her obsessional program. This new self will be unencumbered by "crude events" like menstruation (starving stops her period) and the "filthy details" of either sexual relations or childbirth. The self which she sets out to create will manage all the demands associated with today's grown-up woman by not growing up. She can feel free and secure only by avoiding adulthood and simply remaining a child.

Why are there so many anorexic girls today? Why is the anorexic personality today what the hysteric was in Freud's time? Among the many possible answers to these questions has to be the new demands placed on women. The increased choices open to a woman increases the pressures on her to achieve. In addition, girls today mature earlier. Unexpected physical development might catch some sensitive creature unready emotionally for the female body changes and their implications. She may very well be pushed along socially to date and may have been frightened by a boy's kiss or embrace. The pornographic pictures which now circulate so freely can also cause her to be afraid. Any number of different events or experiences may contribute to this sad and dangerous personality disorder.

Anorexia nervosa may seem like a bizarre new form of emotional disorder, but in fact it is more like a new twist on a very old problem. The anorexic girl is afraid. She struggles to find a safe way of being in the world. The world threatens to overwhelm her, and she tries to adjust by constructing a personality which will keep her frightened feelings under control.

Another personality construction which qualifies both as illness and characteristic of our age is narcissism or a narcissistic personality disorder. If both the anorexic and the alcoholic reflect in their personality disorders certain aspects of our twisted culture, the same is true of narcissism. The seventies and eighties are understood by many different thinkers as a time of turning toward the self. People concentrate on their belly dancing, their jogging, their eating, their pleasures, and on and on. As self-attention reaches epidemic proportions, some persons adopt these "typical" behaviors in exaggerated form. When exaggerated self-centeredness becomes an integral part of the personality then we get instances of a narcissistic personality disorder. For such a person the wide world is shrunken to the dimensions of the self, or individual needs and interests are inflated to become the whole world. Self-absorption is joined to delusions of grandeur to create a now common emotional disorder.

The personality profile of a narcissistic disorder is full of paradox and apparent contradiction. Alongside grandeur and an appearance of omnipotence there is a weak self-esteem and an unhealthy dependence on others. The narcissistic personality is independent and freed from family or any other kind of ties, but is at the same time dependent upon others for a sense of significance. Without their adulations he cannot stand. The very grandiosity of the narcissist is a compensation for deep-seated feelings of insecurity. He is attached to persons who radiate the power and celebrity he needs, but the attachment is never such as to lead to real intimacy or caring. (Others are more mirrors than persons.) The other side of egomaniacal grandiosity and aloof independence is an infantile and empty self. It is this very contradiction that constitutes the disorder of this personality structure. The narcissistic personality is a disorder because the absence of real relationships creates a dreadful and terrorizing isolation.

A narcissistic personality may have sexual involvements, but they are devoid of real feelings. Because of inner weakness and deep-seated insecurity the narcissist is afraid to feel. If feelings surface at all they tend to be negative (rage, hostility, anger, aggression) rather than positive ones (love, satisfaction, creativity, altruism). Repeated sexual gratifications neither satisfy nor fill up the inner emptiness. If anything brings this disordered personality to therapy it will be complaint of feeling empty or perhaps a decline in sexual attractiveness. On the surface, he or she may function very well, perhaps becoming a rich and successful entrepreneur. But just below the surface at the center of the personality there is a dark, soggy hole.

Not every egoist, however, can be considered to be suffering from a narcissistic personality disorder. Emotional disorder is synonymous with exaggerated and costly coping devices, and only an unfortunate minority get caught in the most ineffectual and costly strategies of narcissism. The common, ordinary, run-of-the-mill egoist may not be a very happy person or very pleasant to be around, but he cannot be said to be suffering from a serious personality disorder. He or she in fact may have a fairly accurate self-understanding which is usually missing in more serious personality disorders.

But there are enough personality disorders to cause alarm. The seriously ill narcissistic personality is one of the most common forms of emotional affliction today, and it shows up important aspects of our age. Like the alcoholic and the anorexic, the narcissist and his behavior write out in large print the story of our times and the story of millions of "healthy" persons. If we pay attention to common forms of emotional problems we can learn a lot about ourselves and narcissistic personality disorder tells us more about ourselves than most other contemporary forms of affliction. If people generally in our culture are less human because of their isolation from others, especially those others who are suffering and needy, then the narcissistic personality with its exaggerated isolation is a sign of our times writ large. What is talked about as our current cult of personality is the public image of a widespread weakening of healthy personality structure. Not to be able to care for others is a very serious problem because it makes impossible the continuation of the species.

This disorder like so many others has its roots in the earliest stages of life. Freud called attention to a narcissism that is part of the development of every child. The infant for example does not distinguish self from world. In the beginning the world is the self. Associated with this infant self-centeredness is both a grandiosity and a sense of omnipotence. All the baby needs to do is cry, and magically every need is satisfied. As the infant develops, however, other persons are recognized as distinct from the self, and a certain amount of dissatisfaction or frustration has to be endured. But if separation from mother and all the other painful emotional experiences associated with growth are too much to handle, the child may cope by creating omnipotent images of himself and forming his personality according to this unrealistic idol. Anger and hostility which are generated by disappointment and trauma may be managed by repression which creates pools of negative emotions that underlie this particular disorder. The narcissistic personality is a complicated disorder, but it can be understood as a coping device for handling massive early disappointment which is always associated with hostile and aggressive feelings. When the mother-infant relation does not go well, there will be both feelings of rage and clumsy defenses for managing them.

The narcissistic personality may have origins not all that different from the anorexic and the alcoholic, but it manifests itself differently. Rather than the well-defined symptoms of alcohol abuse or self-starvation, the narcissist shows only diffuse and unspecific dissatisfactions. His complaints will be of vague discomforts: feelings of futility or purposelessness in life, feelings of inner emptiness or depression, an inability to form deep friendship, violent oscillations of self-esteem, grandeur, and omnipotence, on the one hand, then panic and emptiness in the absence of adulation. Just below the surface of what may appear from the outside to be a smooth but aloof person are deep pools of rage requiring a cluster of defensive strategies which become identified with a personality. The narcissist may look healthier than the alcoholic and the anorexic, but looks in this case are deceiving.

The narcissist is facile at manipulating a public image and works hard engineering adulation but forms no bond with those on whom he depends for his feelings of esteem. In fact he is actually contemptuous of his admirers. He cannot get enough of their applause because no amount of it will appease his emptiness and insecurity. Aging and death fill the narcissist with panic, and the world is perceived as full of threatening objects. Wild egomania and unrealistic self-importance are costly and ineffective defenses against deep-seated feelings of terror.

Costly and ineffectual forms of adjustment are the more noticeable the more they resemble the unusual behaviors of the hooked trout which attracts the attention of every other fish in the vicinity. One personality may resort to public drunkenness and make headlines in the evening paper. Under the same stress, another may withdraw into private depression and starvation. Both types of behaviors are expensive, painful, and unproductive. These may be just passing behaviors or they may become so deep-seated that they can constitute a personality dysfunction.

Returning to the analogy of the car, it is not the personality which climbs the hills and purrs smoothly down the road which attracts our attention. Rather we notice the one which lacks the power to make a hill or makes all kinds of unpleasant noises. It is the broken-down car which invites examination. Personalities, like motors, have a certain amount of inner power. There are periods when they start running rough and require tuning, and sometimes they break down entirely.

The badly tuned personality is one that has lifelong problems with living. As the environment becomes more difficult and stressful negative feelings increase. But even in normal times there are problems with relationships, job, and the satisfaction of basic needs. Such personalities simply cannot find an adequate adjustment, and their characteristic way of behaving are either self-defeating or ineffectual or difficult for others to stand.

If the repeated failures and disturbance and dissatisfactions were recognized as resulting from an inadequate personality style, the personality could be worked on and changes might be brought about. But characteristically, difficulties and disruptions in life are ascribed to someone or something outside. In personality disturbances, expensive and ineffective adaptive mechanisms have become so wedded to the personality that they are noticed by everyone except the person using them.

How can a person tell whether his or her personality or personality style is healthy? If the reader had time to study the literature of psychiatry he would find many forms of disturbed or pathological personalities listed.[3] And if one had time to look into the description of each form of personality disorder he would probably be shocked to find something about himself included under each of the different pathological categories.

But this does not mean that everyone suffers from a personality disorder. Viewing emotional affliction as a form of maladjustment or a disturbance in the relation between a person and his environment (trout metaphor) means that every personality has problems from time to time. The emotionally ill personality is not some queer, other-worldly being, but someone like us; someone who uses the same tactics we use to control painful negative feelings, but goes a little too far or gets stuck in one particular type of bad coping device. We all have emotional problems, and sometimes we are very much like the emotionally afflicted person. Usually, however, the "normal" person moves back from the costly and crazy behaviors while the emotionally afflicted person gets stuck in them. The difference between health and illness is a matter of persistence of costly behaviors and the degree to which these become wedded to the personality.

Rather than being someone set apart the emotionally afflicted person is different from the rest only in degree. Emotional health and illness belong on a sliding scale. At one end is the state of adjustment. At the other extreme is the most severe maladjustment. And all of us move back and forth along this scale. The fortunate among us move away from the costly and unproductive management devices for our bad feelings as soon as the stress is reduced. The less fortunate get stuck at a point on the scale or make some ineffectual device part of their personality structure.

If emotional problems are not rooted in some degenerative physical cause, then more than likely they are a temporary disorder and not a hopeless situation. People who become disturbed in the sense of losing their emotional balance can get better. Sometimes in fact they get better all by themselves. Costly, ineffective, and hurtful coping devices can be recognized for what they are and more constructive ways of handling feelings can be adopted. Even personalities can be changed. Some change as a result of change in living conditions. Others show the result of great effort expended on self-improvement. Most change as a result of a good intimate relationship. A small percentage improve as a result of the efforts of professional people who help them to understand what is happening. Understanding is like magic. Even when a behavior is integrated into a personality it can be turned around by understanding and discipline.

8. *People who drive other people crazy*

What makes a personality disorder different from other forms of emotional affliction is the integration of an unusual coping device into the very structure of a personality. Consequently the affliction is more apparent to others than it is to the person suffering from it. Coping devices like phobias and compulsions are experienced as painful and foreign to the person but not so the symptoms of a personality disorder. In this case the ineffectual coping devices become a "natural" part of the self. When this happens anxious feelings do not play a prominent role, and repeated life disturbances associated with the use of costly strategies are either excused or blamed on environmental factors.

Personality disorders are like frozen solutions to certain negative feelings, and there are as many personality disorders as there are bad solutions to painful emotions. Different psychiatric theorists have their own lists and some are longer than others. They extend from the most general categories like the inadequate personality which refers to awkward and inept persons who bungle through life, to antisocial or criminal personalities who habitually relieve feelings by striking out at society. The infantile personality refers to the baby-doll type strategy with its calculated facade of helplessness. (Typically she expects to be able to do anything she wants, whenever the fancy strikes her. She expects to be forgiven because she remains so childlike. How can this be understood as hostility? Just look at the embarrassment, indeed humiliation, caused to the husband and the expense incurred by her inability to manage responsibility.) Cyclothymic is a fancy tag for moody personalities which fluctuate between very positive and very negative feeling states. Hysterical personalities are always acting out their feelings and seemingly unaware of their behavior. Negativistic personalities are frozen into a "no" response and cannot either give anything to others or permit themselves any satisfaction. In every case, the coping device employed to accommodate the threatening feelings becomes joined with one's personality so that it is experienced as a "natural" way of being.

To get a clear idea about personality disorders, let's look more closely at a common personality type that drives other people crazy. It is sometimes referred to as a passive-aggressive personality. The characteristic features of a personality disorder are nowhere more in evidence than with this particular personality style. Like other forms of emotional affliction, this disorder is characterized by an intense feeling of hostility which in this case is expressed indirectly and in a somewhat disguised manner. Aggression is healthy and normal when it is directed against a threat to one's person or belongings. The capability of responding to evil in an effective way is part of a healthy personality structure. When, however, feelings of aggression and hostility are not in response to real attack but rather are diffuse within the person and indiscriminate in their expression, then something is wrong. There is nothing natural about seething in anger and hostility for long periods of time. When diffuse and enduring hostility manifests itself passively rather than in direct forms, then we have an example of passive-aggressive personality structure.

Take the situation in which a boss issues an order to do something unpleasant which irritates an employee and triggers off the ever-present feelings of hostility. If the worker has a passive-aggressive personality he does not let the boss know what he is feeling. Rather he says nothing, but carries out the order half-heartedly, and with constant complaining. He procrastinates rather than getting right to work, spending a lot of time and energy getting around the job rather than accomplishing it. Stubbornness, showing up late, foot-dragging, complaining, criticizing, generalized noncompliance—these are characteristic devices used by the personality to manage underlying negative feelings. They drive others to anger, rather than expressing anger directly. In this personality disorder feelings of aggression always come out passively and indirectly.

This particular style sometimes reaches clinical intensities, but it is frequently found in subclinical forms. Children frequently use these tactics, and it is almost typical of adolescents who are asked to do some work. Even in these lesser forms it causes anger, frustration, and hostility in others, as any parent will readily attest.

The full-blown version of this disorder in adults means consistently passing up healthier ways of feelings management in favor of the passive-aggressive response. The employee we referred to could have refused the order and avoided the unpleasant task, or he could have made the best of it and won approval for his work. Compromise, or reaching some understanding about work conditions, is an example of a healthier coping strategy which is rejected or ignored. The typical passive-aggressive response is to do the unpleasant task grudgingly, to lose the boss's approval, and to leave the work situation unchanged. It is the worst possible solution to an emotionally upsetting situation.

As one can imagine, the passive-aggressive personality runs into constant difficulty in work situations. But in intimate relationships the coping devices of his personality style are even more self-defeating. They are as good an example as one can find of behavior which is motivated by feelings of aggression and is at the same time extremely costly and self-defeating.

During the summer, a man comes home from work looking forward to nine holes of golf after supper. His wife has her heart set on going to a movie. The passive-aggressive type person would take her to the movie, but do so grudgingly. He would drag his feet getting away, arrive late, pout during the show, complain afterwards about the waste of time, and succeed thereby in ruining the evening. The behaviors he exhibits are motivated by anger and hostility. And his coping strategies make everyone else angry. The coping behaviors could not be more self-defeating and costly if they were designed to be so.

Although everyone uses passive-aggressive tactics on occasion, the passive-aggressive personality gets stuck in this behavior. As he or she grows older, life becomes more and more unsatisfying both at work and in personal relations. These persons find themselves with no friends and socially isolated. In addition, the pent-up feelings of anger and hostility take an awful toll on their bodies. Starting with the weakest system (gastrointestinal tract in one person, nervous system in another), the negative feelings gradually produce multiple somatic complaints. In its most intense form, this personality style constitutes a serious problem. If illness causes pain and keeps the sufferer from a normal productive life, then the passive-aggressive personality is definitely ill.

9. *People dangerous to others and to themselves*

Some people with personality disorders vent their hostility and hate on themselves, while others direct feelings of hostility toward strangers or hatred toward society. Formerly these persons were called morally insane or moral degenerates. In ordinary language they might be called perverse or dangerous criminals. In psychiatric language a hardened and incorrigible criminal who compulsively directs hostile feelings against society may be diagnosed as suffering from an antisocial personality.

Criminals who fit the characteristics of this personality disorder (perhaps one-fourth) often do not fit the standard images people have of criminals. They tend not to be ugly, but good looking, and oftentimes have good manners as well. Average or above average intelligence and good physical builds are also common. And yet there is something disturbing about their way of interacting with people, and there is a continuing imbalance in their adjustment to the environment. They lack what we often refer to as standard ethical sensitivities and seem irresistibly drawn to crime.

Aside from their criminal propensities, these persons come across as attractive, even charming characters. They have none of the physical disabilities of the sickness-prone personality and none of the fears or hangups of the alcoholic. Beneath a pleasant and normal surface, however, there are the same pools of hatred and hostility which characterize the other forms of emotional affliction. In the process of expressing hatred and hostility toward society, however, this personality also hurts itself. There is a thin line between self and others, and where powerful negative emotions are involved the damage inevitably spills over from one to the other. Criminal personalities are at one and the same time self-destructive and destructive of society's laws and values.

One of the features of this style which is shared by other personality disorders is the maddening repetitiveness of the self-defeating behaviors. Over and over again the sufferer repeats the same costly and ineffectual gestures causing pain to himself and others. In this sense there is a "stupidness" about this and every personality disorder. The sufferers seem immune to learning. In the antisocial personality this sad trait shows itself when the criminal finally leaves prison after years of suffering and immediately does the same thing that landed him there in the first place. In some cases, in fact, one cannot escape the conviction that such personalities just can't wait to be punished. Otherwise the dumb moves that guarantee getting caught cannot be explained.

The type of crime committed by this form of personality need not be violent and the person need not be fully grown. Sometimes even children suffer from this personality disorder. The son of a minister, for example, from a very early age, stole from the collection plate, pilfered the clothing of Sunday worshipers, and in fact stole everything he got his hands on. He stole at home, at school, at church retreats, everywhere. And he never felt the slightest guilt. It was difficult for anyone to believe that he was a thief because of his otherwise exemplary behavior. Not unlike older criminals, he didn't know why he stole, and underlying this odd behavior were the same pools of negative feelings. Anger and hostility were released through the behavior of stealing.

Although there is a statistical predominance of men in this personality category, there are plenty of women who suffer from the illness. Some few are violent criminals. Most find outlets for their underlying hostile emotions in theft, promiscuity, con schemes, and the like. Their personal lives usually involve a litany of bad marriages, divorces, rapes, and sado-masochistic adventures. And yet to meet some of these women one would find it hard to believe that a physically attractive and apparently intelligent woman could have had such a personal history. Characteristically, however, she feels neither guilt nor remorse for her behavior.

One of the clearest examples of this disorder I have known personally was a man serving a long prison term for multiple murders. Before this particular jail sentence he had served time for robbery, assault, and rape. His problems with the law, he said, went back to grammar-school days, when he stole at school and from his parents. He was at the time I knew him still a fairly young man, even younger in looks than his actual years. He had a baby face, dressed very neatly, and showed good manners. It was only when conversations turned to his criminal activities that the personality disorder showed itself. When asked about the rapes and robberies, he would describe them in a flat unemotional tone and could provide few specific details about his criminal deeds. The murders for which he had been convicted were gruesome acts. In one case they involved killing a mother and three of her children. In another case he beat an old man unconscious and then ran over him with a car. But he claimed to have no feelings about any of these crimes. He said, "I felt nothing at the time and feel nothing now. It just happened." There was no guilt, no remorse, no sense of what the victims felt or any concern about them as people. If some degree of ethical development is required for both moral and emotional maturity, he lacked this entirely. Despite his denial, however, he was full of angry and hostile feelings which he handled by committing terrible crimes.

Sometimes dangerous or antisocial personalities can be helped to grow ethically and to find less destructive ways of managing their negative feelings. Sometimes a special talent will help a person to overcome the most destructive features of his personality. Some famous generals showed perverse characteristics in their youth but were able to modify these enough to avoid a life of crime because of a special talent. And military life is not the only outlet. Any career or profession can provide healthy outlets for potentially unhealthy feelings of hostility. It doesn't take much imagination to picture the composer Richard Wagner as a criminal. He was cruel and manipulative and did terrible things to people without the least show of remorse. But he was able to avoid the worse recriminations of society because of his musical talent. Genius guaranteed his freedom and his productivity gave him social acceptance. The less talented, full of the same emotions, fill our jails and prisons.

The prominence of hostility and aggression in psychopaths is such that no one can miss it. Attacking and hurting literally dominate their lives. Beneath the superficially adult and attractive exterior is an ugly childish preoccupation with getting back. Pools of hate, often unknown to the criminal, motivate both his unlawful acts and his self-destructiveness. Enormous talent may modify these negative feelings enough to avoid the worst consequences. A war may provide an outlet for them and even create an occasional hero. Frequently a talented therapist will be able to educate a person's ethical sensitivities. For the most part, however, the dangerous person lives out life with his personality disorder. He never gets over this emotional disorder which means that widespread suffering follows him wherever he goes.

The Sickness-Prone Personality

Everyone knows that stressful situations and failures of adjustment sometimes cause physical symptoms. All doctors are aware that certain disorders (such as heart attacks) frequently cause psychological symptoms. And physical problems such as asthma, headaches, colitis, and skin diseases are sometimes caused by emotional disorders. But in fact, any kind of physical symptom can result from emotional and psychological causes. Just as some people are accident prone and repeatedly hurt themselves, others are illness prone and continually fall ill. The constancy with which one physical problem follows another leads to a suspicion that there is an underlying reason for all the sickness. This reason may escape the conscious awareness of the sufferer, but can often be exposed by a careful psychological analysis. There may even be an unconscious wish to be sick. Becoming sick brings with it secondary benefits and is a good example of a bad way of handling negative feelings. The need for sympathy and attention is a major factor in this personality style. In any event, after it lasts a certain time one can talk of a personality disorder in the sense of a continuing and repeated pattern of handling emotional upsets by becoming physically ill.[4]

The sickness-prone personality is not only always sick, but even during periods of relative symptom-relief, sickness is the main topic of conversation. Life literally centers around his or her symptoms. Because the physical symptoms play such a dominant role in the life of such a person, psychiatrists assume that they have an important psychological function. They are used as coping devices for bad feelings.

One woman started developing physical symptoms soon after getting married. She was so sick with headaches that she could not take care of her home. Her weakness kept her from doing the shopping and cooking. She was so tired at night that she could not engage in sexual relations. She was so nervous that she could go nowhere with her husband. The only place she managed to get to was the doctor's office, and she went from one to another in search for a cure of her many physical problems. Finally a psychiatrist suggested that she had all kinds of negative feelings about her marriage and that being sick had become her way of handling them. He recommended that she separate from her husband and live alone for one month to see if any of her ailments were relieved. She did so and felt greatly improved during that time. But she returned to her husband and to her ailments and carried a lifelong grudge against the psychiatrist who had put his finger on the ineffectual solution she had adopted for handling her feelings of anger and disappointment.

Proving that emotions cause changes in the body is a good example of proving the obvious. When the emotions are negative and more or less continuous, one can easily imagine how they cause serious physical problems. Passing emotions cause transitory body changes, and persistent negative emotions cause the chronic physical ailments characteristic of the psychosomatic personality. The important message of Norman Cousins in "Anatomy of an Illness" is that positive emotions can do the opposite; i.e., sometimes cure an incurable physical illness. A later book by Cousins offers more scientific proof of what is a convincing intuitive hypothesis about the relation of emotion, health, and illness.

The body's primary defense against disease (immune system) is very susceptible to emotional upset. When stress and its corresponding emotions are prolonged, the efficiency of the immune system is diminished, and many different kinds of real physical illness can result. People commonly think that if the cause is emotional, the physical illness is imaginary or "all in the head." As a matter of fact, negative feelings cause real disease. The sickness-prone personality may sometimes stage sickness or invent imaginary sickness, but may also be really sick.

This personality disorder uses both real and imaginary sickness to communicate a message: "Take care of me," "Don't leave me." Psychiatric help for such a personality would provide an understanding of the function of the inef-

-fective coping devices being used and gradual training in other more effective ways of handling one's feeling states.

10. Aloof, detached, and terrified personalities

Schizoid is the fancy technical term for someone who in ordinary language may be called aloof or detached. Some terrified people manage their feelings by withdrawing. They come across as separate or perhaps a bit strange. There is a tenuousness about their relationships that is quickly picked up even in a casual acquaintance.

The schizoid is a very complicated personality disorder. It is difficult to understand, and yet it is considered to be one of the characteristic afflictions of our time. Freud saw many hysterical personalities in his practice. The psychiatrist today sees many aloof or schizoid personalities. A typical contemporary patient does not feel comfortable around other people and if anyone insists on getting behind his social facade the underlying terrified feelings increase to the point of panic. Day-dreaming and fantasies of being rich and powerful play a big role in the management of his fears and insecurities.

Schizoid personalities show up primarily in relationships. Their emotions are shallow and they tend to experience others with suspicion. Although they are emotionally withdrawn they sometimes develop a smooth social adaptation. In fact the very characteristics of shallow emotion and aloofness may constitute an advantage for some types of work. An aloof and detached person may be successful as an executive because he is able to do things to people without being enough in touch with them to be bothered by the consequences of his acts.

Under what may appear to be a certain kind of strength is a deeply buried personality flaw which splits off this type of person not only from feeling relationships with others, but even from the feeling aspects of his own life. Schizoid means split in Greek, and in this context it refers to a person being split off from deep emotions and feelings within the self. Some schizoid personalities pursue sensual stimulation without emotional involvement as a way of ignoring or refusing to confront emotional deficits. Others withdraw even from sensation and try to achieve a kind of emotional numbness. Disengagement, detachment, aloofness, emotional uncommittedness, and superficiality become the core of a personality style which is threatened by feelings of insecurity and uses all the above devices for handling those feelings.

One way to describe the aloof and detached personality is to say that he tries to convert his life into a smoothly running machine. Life in the sense of emotional relationship to other people is messy, unpredictable, threatening, insecure, and frequently painful. In place of relationships and deep emotion, distance and emotional numbness are substituted as coping devices. After a while these coping strategies become wedded to the self. By adopting such a strategy the person can concentrate all energy on some type of professional or occupational productivity. Protected from time-consuming emotional involvements, more work is possible, which spells success. Some of the great world figures, if not full-blown schizoid personalities, had schizoid features to their personalities.

Woodrow Wilson, for instance, gained the presidency after having been a chief executive in a major university and the governor of a state. But in each of those positions his characteristic style was that of aloofness from his colleagues and detachment from his advisors. As a child he was never close to other children. There is not sufficient reason to say that Wilson was schizoid in the sense of a full-blown personality disorder. The evidence indicates only that his personality has schizoid features. Just recently, in fact, letters were published which showed him to have been capable of intense sexuality and real feelings of intimacy with at least one other person. He died alone except for his wife.

There were similar features in Napoleon's personality. He, too, was shy and unsociable as a child, playing alone rather than with friends. His instructors described him as reserved, haughty, quiet, egotistical, and a lover of solitude. In his case, a sense of superiority provided justification for his aloofness. The successes which he enjoyed early on were definitely associated with his solitariness. But ultimately, as with Wilson, the schizoid features took their toll. Napoleon too died lonely and friendless.

These examples are of schizoid-like personalities who were probably saved from severe personality disorders by exceptional talent. The most pathetic examples of this form of disorder are found in persons who have little or no talent and little chance of modifying their costly, but embedded coping strategies. They go through life alone, afraid, and without the gratification of either power or prestige or personal satisfaction.

What does this personality style have to do with feelings of aggression and hostility, and why is it considered a form of emotional disorder? It seems more like an expression of fear or insecurity, and it is. But where there is fear and insecurity can aggression and hostility be far behind? How do people who are insecure and afraid respond? With some form of aggression. This whole personality style in fact is an act of aggression against the self. The real self of the schizoid is killed. The characteristic tactic of this personality disorder is to deal death to a segment of the person much like a rat chews off his foot in order to save the rest of himself. Fear and hate are closely bonded in the schizoid. It is interesting to note how much violence and bloodshed resulted from the policies of Wilson and Napoleon.

Drug use, too, is frequent, especially in the less famous young schizoid persons whom psychiatrists see so often today. Drugs provide an artificial feeling state for someone who has become dead within. Oftentimes a young person will say that he uses drugs in order to experience closeness to another person. Looked at more carefully, many of these temporary intimacies are not at all what they are interpreted to be. Drugs are ways of generating feeling, but they have their effects without other people. They are more a continuation of the characteristic distance from others than a way of getting close. Most drugs increase estrangement rather than overcome it. And they have the added unconscious advantage of expressing aggression and violence against the self—a sort of controlled suicide.

The story of one young man, Bill, puts the meaning of drug abuse by schizoid personalities in very concrete terms. He felt shy and uncomfortable around other people for as long as he could remember. In middle school he started smoking dope, at first as a way of being accepted and later, because it "made him feel good." The good feeling was more than anything else a relief from the ever-present discomfort he felt around people.

Under increasing pressure in high school to have a girlfriend, he established a relationship with a young lady who had a reputation for using drugs. They smoked hash on their first date and later started experimenting with other drugs, especially acid. Again he felt that the drugs helped him feel closer to his girlfriend, but later on he realized that the drugs were increasing his distance from her and other people.

His drug use continued in college. Now he was able to generate added reasons for using hallucinogens: to be in contact with ultimate reality; to expand his experience; to increase his capacity of deep insight. During this period he added many other drugs and sometimes would take a number of them indiscriminately. Despite the rationalizations he became increasingly aware of the fact that he was blowing his mind.

His drug use gave Bill an experience of being split up or fragmented and at the same time gave him a certain detachment from this frightening state. The drug-induced experience of fragmentation and detachment not only symbolized his personality, but increased its features. He was terrified by his sense of being split off from others and being split up within himself into many warring parts. Drugs increased his schizoid experience but also made it possible for him to endure its terror. One of his pastimes was to get stoned and watch horror films. *Clockwork Orange* was one of his favorites, and he saw it more than fifty times. The conflicted and violent main character of the film he easily identified with. Getting stoned and watching this story was his way of handling his personal fears about life. By using drugs during the show he made all the terror seem far away.

By the time he got through college he was an emotional and physical wreck. Everything terrified him. He felt as though everyone and everything could engulf and destroy him. His defense was to remove himself farther than ever from his own life.

Bill, and other young schizoid personalities, put their real self into a separate cold storage in order to keep it safe. They feel weak and helpless, split apart and isolated, lonely and terrified of closeness, afraid yet hostile to the point of being willing to destroy themselves by their behaviors. Again, if an affliction is what causes pain, disrupts life, and incapacitates a person, then a schizoid personality is an affliction.

Bill's personality disorder and schizoid personalities generally have their origin in attempts to manage painful feelings. As we have mentioned before, emotional disorders in this and other forms are bizarre sets of behaviors developed to cope with feelings which are painful and threatening. Like the trout, the human being who feels caught and terrified adopts unusual gestures to seek relief. The sense of being caught arouses aggression and hostile feelings which are ever-present in the human being and always in danger of getting out of control.

To understand emotional disorders, then, we look for threatened unbalance and for feelings of hostility. We focus on destructiveness and self-destruction. The many forms of emotional distress are variations on these themes. Usually it is easier to see these features in others than it is to recognize them in ourselves. But we are all prone to these behaviors, and we all suffer the consequences of aggression and hostility when it becomes intense or gets out of control.

In fact, if we look carefully most of us can see aspects of all the personality disorders we have been discussing in our own personality. The cause of emotional afflictions is present in doctors and poets, grocers and politicians, scientists and priests. Given the right conditions, they can come to the surface in the form of destructive, ruthless, cruel, and lawless feelings and in behaviors adopted to cope with them. We all act downright crazy on occasion. On occasion we all adopt behaviors engineered by feelings of hostility which are not a response to any impending threat. Emotional affliction is a matter of degree, and what follows in the next section is a sketch of how a person can move from one costly and ineffective coping device to another and in the process can become more and more disturbed.

II. LEVELS OF HEALTHY AND UNHEALTHY FUNCTIONING

1. Healthy emotional life—a matter of smart tactics

In all the examples we have used up to this point, the living environment and emotional balance become so disturbed that the person cannot adjust with the use of standard coping devices. Emergency measures are called for. In some cases these measures alter the environment. In other cases the feelings themselves are altered in order to achieve some adaptation. If, however, either the self or the environment become too distorted in this process, then we have an instance of emotional disorder. Emotional health understood in negative terms is the absence of such disorders. For the person who enjoys emotional health, life may be so gentle that no serious disturbances occur in the environment, or the self may be so gifted and strong that it is able to control the ever-changing feelings without getting twisted in the process.

Emotional health and illness are different ways of reacting to problems and we all have both to some degree. Some behaviors or forms of response are healthier than others. Even people who consider themselves healthy at times adopt behaviors that qualify as ill or pathological. One standard for drawing the distinction between one and other type behavior is adaptation or balance. Another standard is a capacity to work and to get along with other people. Good emotional health then can be understood as a matter of smart tactics for achieving this treasured balance and adaptation. More specifically good emotional health depends upon the following: a sense of humor, courage, honesty, spontaneity of action, social responsibility, understanding one's past and accepting

90

it, reaching goals, being able to love and to work. But no one can go along just doing these healthy and upbeat kinds of things. Disturbances on the outside or within the self cause negative feelings to become dominant. Negative feelings in turn require that the person come up with emergency management devices which may or may not be costly and inefficient.

Negative feelings threaten a person's equilibrium (in the sense of his normal adaptation to surroundings) and force the employment of re-balancing behaviors or coping devices. We all experience those feelings because unpleasantness, conflict, and upsetting things are always around the corner. Conflicts can develop between us and significant other persons, between our self-image and the way we come across to others, between our conscience and our behavior. There is literally no end to the areas of conflict, and unexpected things just keep happening. Consequently, negative feelings can and do threaten to overwhelm us, and we are forced to come up with emergency coping mechanisms. The coping devices people use are as important as genes and biochemistry in determining whether they stay emotionally healthy.

Let me illustrate this point by telling a little story about myself. Sunday afternoon I usually dedicate to the task of reading the *New York Times,* made even more enjoyable when it is raining and I wouldn't be tempted to go out. On just such a Sunday I had settled into my favorite chair and was halfway through the book review section when the phone rang. It was my teenage daughter. She had asked to borrow the car, and now she was calling to tell me that she was stuck at the entrance to a busy intersection.

I dropped everything, changed clothes, and called a friend to accompany me on the rescue mission. As I did all this, I could feel the angry feelings mounting. Putting on my coat, I made a few remarks to my wife about kids and cars and the trouble they cause.

My expectation was that it would be something simple and that I would soon be back to the paper. But it didn't quite work that way. None of the standard moves were successful. The car just wouldn't start. Since it could not be left where it was, I had to walk to a service station in order to have the car towed.

The attendant is a naturally gruff and disagreeable person who becomes downright aggressive around college professors. (More than likely he has had some unpleasant experiences with them, and *his* negative feelings rise with every renewed contact.) After a long wait, he got around to me, and we set out together to rescue my wounded carriage. The trip was made in silence. Upon arrival he made some remarks about the age of my car. As he begun the towing operation, he shouted military-style orders to me about what to do and what not to do. If I didn't carry out each command exactly to his liking, he let me know about it and then impatiently did it himself.

Back at the station, I asked about the charge. Without looking at me, he threw the keys to his attendent and said I would be getting one big bill for the tow and the repair.

Anger and frustration had mounted at each stage of the process, and by the time I left the station I was tense as well as a little embarrassed. The helplessness of the situation and my own inability to manage it more adroitly intensified the negative feelings.

Driving home with my friend, I began employing my first management device—I talked. I expressed my anger about the garageman's behavior. I blamed everything on his boorish manners. When I got home, I released more of the feelings by more talk, this time with a few expletives not used in polite society. And yet I still felt uptight.

Next, I contacted another garage and made arrangements to have someone else do the repair work. Taking that initiative meant regaining some control and relieving some of my feeling of helplessness. After this, I began to feel a little better.

Instead of going back to the paper, I decided to go out and play a few holes of golf. The sun had come out by that time and flailing at that ball did wonders for my bad disposition. Immediately after the incident it was all I could think about, but at the end of nine holes emotional equilibrium was restored to the point where other more pleasant feelings had been restored. A few beers at the clubhouse provided a context for some jokes about my earlier problems, my feelings, and all the silly things I had said and done. Now, instead of being angry I was laughing at the whole affair.

The incidents surrounding the car had created stress and incited a host of negative aggressive emotions. Talking, acting, playing, drinking, and laughing had reduced the tension and reestablished an emotional balance. In this case, the common coping devices were all that was needed.

But if the disturbance and the stress had been more serious, and if for some reason I did not have access to these standard helping behaviors, I might have harbored the negative feelings or done something ineffective and costly to relieve their pressure.

Behaviors, however, are not like birds, plants, and animals which fall into naturally different groupings. If we presume to designate some behavior as healthy and others as unhealthy, we have to do so on the basis of a scheme or metaphor. Our scheme is adaptation, and one metaphor we have used is that of a hooked fish. The oyster, too, can help us to grasp the subtle difference between healthy and unhealthy ways of handling emotional upsets. The same tensions and conflicts which one person uses to develop pearls of adaptation can cause another only pain and weakness. Some sort of shorthand is required for us to talk intelligently about emotions and coping behaviors.

I already referred to a canoe metaphor to help understand how people become emotionally ill and how close this illness can be to what we accept as normal behavior. The metaphor is worth reading in its entirety.

> Think of a man paddling a canoe downstream. By skillful balance, by holding back his canoe at certain moments, by choosing the most likely channel and using the current where he can, he achieves his purpose and remains alive and comfortable. He encounters sharp turns, overhanging branches, threatening rapids, but by skillful adaptive steering and paddling, he passes them safely.
>
> But for some things ordinary maneuvers will not suffice. A half-submerged log suddenly looms up. A parcel falls from the boat and must be retrieved. His paddle, caught on a rock, snaps in two. The canoe springs a leak or goes aground. For such emergencies special ad hoc steps have to be taken. The time may even come when he has to have help. This need may be apparent from the shore, if anyone is looking, or he may have to spend some of his energy running up distress signals.
>
> The strength or the unexpectedness or the peculiar nature of an external event may upset the relative steady state which was being maintained. Sometimes this is because of special vulnerablities—a thin spot in the boat, a paddle weakened from an earlier exigency. The boatman's extra exertions tire him; they diminish his comfort; they reduce his efficiency. They may exhaust him. He may have to pull over to the shore and temporarily discontinue his voyage; he is "laid up."
>
> But on the other hand, if by special efforts he can rather quickly correct the difficulties and keep going, if he can

shortly resume his old efficiency and speed and confidence and pleasure, we would never consider this minor episode pathological. It was an emergency situation, quickly settled by an emergency maneuver.[1]

The point of this wonderfully clear and concrete story is that there is a certain amount of disruption that has to be expected and what distinguishes a healthy person is the accumulation of many good coping devices to handle inevitable upsets. The emotionally healthy person may not be any stronger than the rest of us but is more aware of his limitations and does not get in over his head. In addition, certain habits of work and play are developed which keep bad feelings and inner tension from accumulating. He has hobbies, love relationships, good friends, may sleep well and dream a lot, is one who can talk easily about things that bother him, and finally may even have a meaningful prayer life. These are examples of very healthy behaviors. A healthy person has his shares of upsets, worried feelings, and upsurges of aggression, but he has a host of good techniques for dealing with them. He channels his hostility into something productive like work or play or a hobby, and he works at developing and maintaining love relationships.

Given the importance of learning to understand and control the aggressive feelings associated with tension, one may wonder why our culture has none of the games and rituals used in other civilizations to teach young persons these all-important lessons. In many places the young people play some version of a game in which one of the many participants tries to incite the other to acts of hostility. One person learns by playing to understand what aggression and hostility are, while the other practices self-control and an ability to control these emotions. Watching television, our young people get just the opposite of good healthy training. They get no practice in using healthy behaviors and, to make things worse, get a very distorted message that hostility is the mark of a hero who dispenses aggression in the primitive tit-for-tat fashion.

Games, play, and the theater provide inexpensive and effective ways of modifying the destructive hostility which lies at the base of serious emotional distress. These are important behaviors for maintaining good emotional health. Some people prefer games like chess or cards; others opt for more physical outlets. A swim or a day of skiing or a game of tennis or a round of golf can do wonders for a person's ability to cope with bad feelings. Some more sedentary types use fantasy or "inner theater" to discharge hostile feelings harmlessly. Eating helps and so too does laughing and crying. A sense of humor and plenty of hearty laughing as we have seen can effect marvelous cures of serious physical disease. But talking out one's feelings is the most common of all healthy devices. The person who does the talking gets the advantage of hearing himself aloud; new ideas occur to him as well as better ways of understanding his emotions. And if someone says something helpful in response, that is an added benefit.

Where other tactics and techniques for coping with feelings of hostility are considered pathological because they are too costly and painful and finally ineffective, the devices mentioned above are considered healthy for the opposite reasons. They keep positive feelings from being squeezed out and maintain a certain satisfying balance between the person and his environment. And the more they are used the stronger and more resilient the person becomes. The expression "to take something in stride" conveys the idea of being able to run into obstacles without stumbling or resorting to bizarre behaviors.

Emotional health, then, is partially at least a matter of using smart tactics for handling feelings, but it is more an ideal to be pursued than a finished accomplishment. The human condition is full of weaknesses which make every person vulnerable at times to inappropriate responses and behaviors. Some people have weak constitutions and are more sensitive than others to the upsets and obstacles. Others, like Anna O., are exposed to too many frightening experiences at a vulnerable time. At crucial periods of development, like infancy, the Oedipal period (age five or six), or adolescence, young people sometimes learn bad techniques for handling feelings which stay with them for years. Perhaps the worst vulnerablility results from such radical deprivation and negative feelings at the beginning of life that normal development simply does not occur. Finally, even with what might be called normal early childhood with its corresponding development, life later on can become too full of obstacles and emotional upsets for anyone to handle in a healthy way.

Rather than talk about emotional health and illness in some absolute sense then, it makes much more sense to talk of more or less mental health and illness. We are all more or less healthy and more or less ill. At some periods we may shift more in one direction than the other. The line between the states is difficult to draw. Certainly we know that some people are ill. They require hospitalization and are commonly referred to as crazy. And many people are so strong that even in very upsetting situations it doesn't take them long to snap back and get adjusted. They are the very healthy. Most of us are somewhere in between. Some hover around boundaries operating either at the edge of normality or just beyond the limit. They are termed odd or nervous or unpleasant to be around. Others have moved from the healthy range by the use of bizarre, costly, and ineffective behaviors. These unfortunate persons are called emotionally disturbed which, among others things, means that they are unable by themselves to get back to the use of more effective coping devices for their negative feeling states.

One way of finding an answer to the question, "Am I emotionally ill?" is to inquire about the techniques you use for handling your negative feelings and upsetting situations. Do your coping devices effect a satisfying adjustment? If they do not, are you stuck with them or can you still change? To help in this self-examination, we will look at the techniques and coping devices arranged in a series from only slightly ineffective or merely odd behavior, to very ineffective and serious forms of emotional distress. Without too much trouble we ought to be able to recognize some of our own typical responses.

2. Ineffectual responses to normal disruptions—forgetting, overworking, substituting, worrying, fantasizing, getting sick: Level I

What are the emergencies or disruptions of normal routine which lead to the call-up of not-so-healthy coping devices? We all know them because they are part of every life. Marital conflicts cause an extraordinary amount of negative emotion. Adolescence all by itself is full of such feelings because it involves so many changes. (If in addition to everything else the adolescent involves himself or herself in intimate relations similar to marriage, then it is almost certain that emergencies will develop and bizarre coping devices will be employed to handle them.) Sometimes people feel unjustly treated by big business. Then there are the many losses that can and do occur: job, health, affection, the death of someone dear. Changing jobs, moving, a financial pinch, these are common and cause all kinds of emotional stress. Even small things like changes in work schedule, or Christmas time, or loss of sleep take their toll.

The response to these emergency situations is increased personal discomfort which sometimes is described as anxiety. More often than not this amounts to an increase in irritability which we often hear referred to as nervousness. No matter how much willpower we use or how much we increase our exercise, the irritablility and tightness do not go away. Despite our best efforts we cry too easily, or fly off the handle at the least provocation, or feel down and depressed. We are emotionally upset.

First there is the emergency situation or disruption in normal routine, followed by the emotional signs of the stress. When the stress and tension persist, we feel upset and we call upon emergency coping devices to reestablish equilibrium or get us back to normal. These coping devices are somewhat helpful and at the same time somewhat unhelpful. They serve a purpose but do so at the price of pain, loss of productivity, and unhappiness. In effect our coping devices constitute the beginning symptoms of what is called emotional affliction. Let's look at some of these.

Forgetting—A person's first response may be the one used by Anna O. If so, balance is maintained in a stressful situation by pushing away awareness of the upsetting situation. The person separates himself or herself from the trouble by a trick of the mind. It is as if an unconscious and automatic device clicks on which gets rid both of unpleasant feelings and the circumstances which cause them. The anger, fear, depression, or hostility is simply forgotten, and the person doesn't allow himself to be conscious either of the experience or the disturbing feelings associated with it. There are many people who need a kind of revelation to know what they are actually feeling or to remember some important event which is associated with the repressed feelings.

Overworking—Some people try to handle a problem with greater amounts of activity. Rather than activity which is effective in altering the situation, however, this activity is characterized by impulsiveness and compulsiveness. The activity is driven and pointless. Some men stay at the office all night and work. Some women clean the house over and over.

Substituting—In every case the stressful situation triggers off aggressive and hostile feelings which are either worked off or are deflected to substitute persons. Sometimes the wife catches hell, or one of the children, and sometimes the poor dog catches an unexpected and angry kick. In the case of the adolescent it is usually the parents who take the brunt of deflected hostile feelings. They are blamed for everything.

Worrying—Rather than act, many people try to cope by thinking. They think through the upsetting situation over and over again. This is called mildly obsessional thinking or worrying. When obsessive thinking joins up to a mild form of activity we know as talking, we get a person everyone tries to avoid at a party.

Fantasizing—Not exactly the same but a coping device related to worry is excessive fantasy formation. Rather than thinking in order to understand the stressful situation or finding ways of altering it, this thinking is characterized by an escape from reality. Young people characteristically use a lot of fantasy to manage feelings, but there are also adults who far too often and too quickly have recourse to this device. They simply remove themselves from troublesome situations by flights of fantasy.

Getting sick—Most people understand that physical ailments associated with emergency situations are caused by tension. It is just as reasonable to see the ailments as coping devices, designed to relieve the bad feelings. Nausea, diarrhea, enuresis, tachycardia, tremors, impotence, and frigidity are on the one hand a result of the vulnerability of the sympathetic nervous system to stress and at the same time attempts to handle the threatened disequilibrium. Very often these symptoms become substitutes for the disturbing situation and managing the symptoms becomes an ineffective way of managing the real emergency.

In summary, then, the emergency or the disruption in our environment causes painful feelings which overtax the person's ordinary adaptational devices. Consequently, extraordinary mechanisms are called symptoms and are interpreted psychiatrically as serving the purpose of managing emotions or reestablishing a disturbed balance.

But symptoms are costly and painful. In some cases they cause more trouble than the original disturbance. Energies are drained, efficiency and satisfactions are reduced, and, worst of all, the down feelings are not relieved. Paradoxically, the coping mechanisms protect people and at the same time increase the very feelings they were designed to relieve. The person employing even these first-level strategies is more a victim than a culprit. He is victimized both by the situation in which he finds himself and by his ways of coping with it. It is as victim that a person qualifies as patient in a psychiatric sense.

The first-level devices are connected to feelings of aggression and hostility in two ways. First, they provide for its expression. Physical symptoms are the most obvious examples of hostility turned against our own bodies: a form of self-punishment. Second, they cause trouble for those who have to listen to us or be around us. Although the connectedness of these devices to hostility and aggression is not always apparent, one need only get behind common-sense explanations to see this ever-present underlying factor. Any upsetting or disrupting situation triggers off unpleasant feelings which then find their way into the devices settled on to cope with them.

Emotional illness in this least serious degree is usually passing. In most cases it is treated by the patient himself. Very often, however, such a person will seek help from a friend or a pastor. The irritating emergency or reason for alarm might go away on its own or, if not, the emotions resulting from it might be mastered without the continued employment of these slightly ineffectual coping devices. A family member, a friend, or a colleague at work may help the victim develop alternate, less harmful, more healthy devices. Nonprofessionals do important therapeutic work. Their interventions are supportive, sometimes insightful, and frequently lead to recovery.

But sometimes things take a turn for the worse. The devices themselves after a while cause more and more discomfort and become less and less effective. The person can become exhausted trying to cope. In addition, the situation may get worse. This will throw the person even more off balance and more extreme devices may be resorted to in order to achieve adjustment. This leads to more serious problems.

3. Withdrawal and the beginnning of more serious forms of emotional illness—fainting, amnesia fugue states, prejudice, fantasies, phobias: Level II

When things get worse it is not just more of the same that a person uses but usually another type of strategy. More serious distress and more costly coping devices have as their common thread a withdrawing from reality. With coping devices at the first level the patient stays in contact with the reality which causes the emotional upset. At this second level, the patient beats a strategic retreat. Now the characteristic of the regulatory devices is partial detachment from reality. You may ask: "What's wrong with getting away from a reality that is threatening? Withdrawal would seem to make perfectly good sense." Well, yes and no. Realistic withdrawal does make good sense in many situations. And there are many instances of natural withdrawal like sleep which are restorative and therapeutic. In the cases we will be discussing, however, it does not relieve the negative feelings and leaves the tension-creating situation exactly as it is.

The simplest example of inner withdrawals are what in psychiatry are called disassociations; i.e., faintings, hypersomnia, amnesia, or fugue states. Not every person who faints, falls asleep at odd times, cannot remember, or walks around in a state of obliviousness, however, is using a more pathological strategy for handling an emotional upset. In fact the first suspicion would be of some physical abnormality. But there are instances in which these same behaviors have no foundation in physiology or anatomy. They are connected to feeling states rather than disruptions of blood supply to the brain. The situation in which a person finds himself is just too overwhelming for his ordinary coping powers, and so he adopts an extraordinary device which provides a brief and partial obliteration of the threat. If the thoughts and feelings which occupied the period of withdrawal could be recovered, we would find that they contained no small amounts of fear and aggression which are controlled by these extraordinary strategies.

(The cases of multiple personality which become the subjects of books, movies, and television shows belong to this same general category of withdrawal, but tend to be much more serious disorders. In the case of Sybil, for example, she withdrew into completely different personalities. Dr. Jekyll and Mr. Hyde is another classical example of handling a troublesome emotional conflict by withdrawing from the real world and creating a different one.)

Some withdrawal strategies are costly and ineffective coping mechanisms constituting second-level disorders while others are perfectly healthy and indeed characteristic of man's unusual way of being in the world. Animals have no choice at all about this matter. They are embedded in narrow realities by necessity. Human beings, because of their unusual capability to step back from their surroundings, are not so determined. Certain forms of withdrawal then are of the very essence of the human and in no way pathological. All science, for example, is a form of withdrawal or detachment from reality in order better to understand it, to symbolize it in numbers, and ultimately to control it. So, too, is sleep. But, like so much of human life, there are healthy as well as unhealthy variations of the same behavior.

In unhealthy or abnormal withdrawal from reality the person loses his bearings. Instead of being better equipped by withdrawal to reattach himself to the world, the person gets stuck in the backward move, thereby creating a vacuum. (It is man's natural condition to be in touch with things and persons.) The human mind naturally involves a moment of withdrawal for reflection, but only to reengage reality more intelligently.

If reengagement does not take place because the reality is too threatening, then a substitute reality is created, one associated with more pleasant feelings. Symbolic objects are substituted for things in the real world which are either too feared or too loved or too hated. We see this human device operating in children with dolls and toys taking the place of real objects and making for easier management of the emotions incited by the real objects. We see it in a less healthy form in prejudice and fanaticism where something symbolic is substituted for the real objects which incite too much fear or love or hate. For example, the person who hates Jews, or Catholics, or blacks, whom he does not know, actually hates some person in his immediate environment or some aspect of himself. The Jew, or black, or Catholic is a symbol or substitute reality. Haters and crusaders are usually doing battle within themselves.

This withdrawing and resymbolizing occurs in many unrealistic attitudes and behaviors. In psychiatry it is called dereism or failure of the person's reality-testing function. Withdrawal, combined with the substituted reality, constitutes a regulatory device for keeping one's balance in the face of what is perceived as unmanageable. Like every such device it provides some benefit, but it comes at a price. Living in withdrawal and with substituted symbolic objects is safer. There are fewer threatening feelings and more pleasant ones, but it is not what human life is all about. In fact, it incapacitates the person using such mechanisms for truly human existence.

The example of prejudice or fanaticism illustrates the technique of substituting one reality for another as well as another tactic known as projection. The new objects not only substitute for the real ones which cause emotional pain, but in the re-creation process all kinds of thoughts and emotions are ascribed to the new objects or projected on to them. As the projected material gets more imaginary or delusional, a greater degree of distress is signaled.

Most people are familiar with the tactic of projecting threatening feelings of one's own onto some ordinarily innocuous object. Every phobia illustrates the process of creating substitute realities and then projecting on to them unfeasible characteristics. Cats take on all kinds of threatening dimensions; numbers like thirteen all of a sudden have destructive powers. There are thousands of phobias because human beings can turn anything into a substitute object. All the fancy Greek terms for different phobias refer to the same behavior of making one thing stand for something else which in reality frightens us.

Persons who get caught in these costly management devices are not paragons of consistency. Like fish who are hooked they shift back and forth between what seem to be rather normal behaviors and altogether abnormal ones. One day they act as though they are in contact with reality, the next they are back to their unrealistic ways. Those who live with such persons are constantly being buoyed up and let down. It is almost as though the disturbed person builds up hopes in order to disappoint and punish.

These second-level coping behaviors are exasperating because they are never completely unrealistic or completely irrational or completely crazy but always only partially so. A common reaction is to want to shake the person using them or slap him into more realistic ways. The reason this "normal" reaction doesn't work is that it is just what this person at some level wants.

Part of the picture of emotional affliction is provocativeness, which is a form of aggression. Rather than expressing hostility in an open and direct form, the provocative person causes the other to be openly and directly hostile. We are all provocative on occasion. Some personalities develop provocativeness as part of their life strategy and then use the results of this tactic to justify their distortions and projections. "I have reason to withdraw," they say in effect. "Look at the horrible way people treat me." Some emotionally disturbed people provoke retaliation and then use the retaliation to justify their withdrawal, distortions, and projections. Their behavior is semirational, semirealistic, perhaps semicriminal. It is this *semi* aspect that makes it so exasperating.

4. Care and its absence in second-level forms of distress

The healthy human person is immersed in an ongoing, give-and-take engagement with his environment, and emotional illness is characterized by variations from this pattern. Subjective withdrawal from the world of real objects and real persons, however, is only part of what it means to be emotionally ill. To be involved in the world in a healthy way is to be in the world with *care*. Loving and caring are not just ethically laudatory or nice ways of being. They are psychiatrically normative, i.e., a requirement for good mental health. There is a point at which not caring is maladaptive and many forms of not caring fall within the second-level forms of emotional illness.

Caring as the hallmark of healthy human being in the world has its roots in man's biology. The human animal requires care for long years in order to be able to survive and gain some independence. To be able to care for another, then, is a biological requisite for species survival. Not to be able to care constitutes a very serious flaw: it is a form of species-impotency. To be able to care but to refuse to do so may be a sin. Not to be able to care, however, is a sign of an emotional problem.

Caring is a peculiarly human phenomenon which has many uniquely human ingredients. A parent's caring for a baby is more than just providing physical sustenance or being interested. It is a way of being related and emotionally involved in the development of another person that is beyond other ways of being together, as loving is beyond liking. It is the unusual relatedness we see in a parent with her child, a teacher with his student, a doctor with his patient. It is something very special.

And at the same time it is a necessary ingredient of authentic and healthy human existence. Caring not only is a directedness toward the other; it is also a proper ordering of one's own life. Caring centers the self, gives order to the activities of one's life and establishes a person's values. Caring gives stability as well as ethical substance to the caring person.

To be realistic and in touch with reality is a hallmark of emotional health. We have seen that the alternative is the beginning of serious emotional illness. It is, however, just as important to be in touch with reality in a caring way. Care gives quality to human connectedness with the outside. Being human in the world has many features: dominating, calculating, manipulating, appreciating, and understanding in addition to caring, but the greatest of these is caring. Only through caring does the human person find his true place among others. To care is to be in contact with reality in a truly human way.

Whether it is for another person that we care, or for his home, or his art, or his environment, or his meanings, or ideals, it is the quality of this relatedness that is important. In caring, the other is recognized as other rather than as part of the self, and as other is loved. This sets caring off from parasitic relations—those morbid forms of dependency which do not have the good of the other or the other's development at heart. It is normal for a child to be radically dependent on another, but when such dependence characterizes adult relations there is distortion of reality. The wife who cannot do anything without her husband or who does not have any sense of herself as an independent person is disturbed. Caring for another is an exercise of will, choice, and freedom, all of which are in short supply in the radically dependent or parasitic person. Symbiotic relationships in which one partner loses himself or herself in the other by becoming nothing may look like very caring unions, but looks here are deceiving. Everything that looks like caring isn't.

Caring is both an expression of a healthy person's being and a behavior that creates healthiness. When a person cares, the other dictates behaviors which require the force of my will to supply in an adequate way. The other's needs emerge as emotional claims on me, and my free response to these claims is an act of strength and personal power. The caring activity may be sensed as obligation or duty at certain times, because the other's needs impose a required set of responses. Ideally, caring is a coming together of what I feel obliged to do with what I want to do. Caring involves the assumption of a burden but one that does not seem to be heavy. "He's not heavy. . . ."

But if caring constitutes both a normal and a necessary way of emotional connectedness to other persons, defects in caring constitute emotional abnormalities and distortions of emotional bonding. Defects of caring, like withdrawals from reality, may be adopted as a way of managing a threatening reality, but such management tactics are too costly and too ineffective to qualify as healthy.

5. Not caring for others—symbolic killing, revenge, self-righteousness

Defects of caring which are serious enough to constitute second-level forms of emotional affliction are legion. Aggressive and angry feelings which have either the self or the other as targets underlie the defects at either extreme. Hostile behaviors are substitute forms of killing rather than caring. Destructive behaviors which are not literal killings are nevertheless symbolic negations of others. Cursing for example does not qualify as pathological, but it is an example of symbolic destruction.

More serious than cursing is revenge, in which a real hurt is planned for another person. Revenge is a serious defect of caring, and people whose lives and energies are taken up with this behavior are more than bitter or sad. They are disturbed. Instances of this type distress can be found in offices as well as homes, courts as well as schools, political institutions, businesses, and yes, even in the church. How much of our all-too-limited life-time and energy is taken up "getting back" or "getting even?" Probably more than we would like to admit.

"Getting back" or "getting even" may inspire what appears on the surface to be a polite remark. Even more than winning, it may also motivate the moves and maneuvers in athletic competition. Sometimes the disguise is subtle, but at other times it is obvious to everyone that what is really going on is a version of tit-for-tat, or an exchange of blows. Not every form of getting back is pathological. It may even be normal at a certain age. But at some point this defect of caring qualifies as an affliction in the sense of costly and ineffective coping behavior.

One of the most popular disguises of revenge is high-sounding moral discourse. A great deal of "getting back" takes the form of "virtuous outrage" at some injury or threat. Pious words and high-sounding rhetoric become a vehicle for indulging the plain old impulse to get back at the hated other. The pious and self-righteous sometimes distinguish themselves by an uncanny capacity to keep alive seething hostility for years. Religious "idealism" and "ethical" demeanor can easily become unhealthy facades for exaggerated hostility.

The next time you waste an evening watching popular television programs, notice how often getting back or getting even makes up the underlying theme of the show. First there is some wrong done, and then a string of events follow which finally even things up. We may give lip service on Sunday to the notion that vengeance is reserved for God, but as a matter of fact we spend a great deal of our lives making sure God doesn't slip up and let some wrong go unaddressed.

The question we have to ask ourselves, however, is whether taking over God's job is all that good for us. Is getting back and getting even a healthy way to live? Or is it in fact a way of inflicting death on ourselves as we inflict justice on others?

One thing is sure: the impulse to get back or get even is one we all recognize. It is known to every child, as well as to every adult. Statistically it can be called normal, and yet there is evidence beyond doubting that in certain intensities it becomes an emotional disorder, serious enough to cause concern. Not only are people killed in order to get even, but suicide too occurs for the same reason.

Human beings, like most animals, have a natural capacity for aggression. There are times when one's territory or home or loved ones must be protected against attack. Only naive persons (like the flower children during the sixties) try to organize their lives on the assumption that there is no evil and, therefore, no reason ever to show aggression.

What makes revenge different is what it adds to aggression. Defensive aggression subsides once the danger is removed. Getting back and getting even continue the aggression long after the situation that stimulated them has subsided. A capacity for aggression is natural to man, but there is nothing natural about continued vindictiveness. Rather, it is unnatural to the point of being a second-level form of emotional disturbance. It distorts human connectedness to reality.

If getting back or getting even is proven to be the cause of much physical and emotional distress, how do we control it in our lives? How can we keep it within bounds? How can we avoid the physical and psychic pain it causes? How can we keep it from becoming one of our standard devices for managing upsets and negative feelings? How can we recognize the situation in which getting back is too costly and therefore, must be left to God for our own sanity?

These are the tasks for a lifetime. It is helpful to be able to recognize revenge for what it is and to realize that it is harmful to good emotional health. But recognition is not the whole answer. Sometimes an ingrained habit has to be changed. Then quiet thought about the example of Jesus Christ may be helpful. He did not get back or get even, and gave his followers a command to initiate the attitude he demonstrated even toward those who hated him. We'll have more to say about managing feelings of revenge in the last section.

When revenge goes beyond the possibility of modification by time and prayer, then we have an instance of more serious emotional disturbance. It is precisely this defect of caring that stands behind the many forms of hurtful, self-defeating, cruel behavior which pollute the human environment. If withdrawal from reality underlies the behaviors which qualify as second-level symptoms of emotional distress, this must be true of revenge. It may not appear so obvious to the layman. but any professional helper who spends time with disturbed people knows how many hang-ups and quirks, how much impotence and unhappiness is rooted in festering preoccupation with getting back at someone. With adolescents who are troubled it is almost always a major component of their problem. All the elements of emotional illness are present: unneutralized aggression, costliness in terms of sacrifice of productivity, ineffectiveness and the impeding of achievement. The revenger's world is less and less involved with open relationships and more and more turned in on himself. Ultimately revenge means isolation, abandonment of reality, and possibly even death.

6. *Not caring for oneself—mutilation, substance abuse, and depression*

Levels or degrees of emotional distress can be identified by attending either to behaviors that can be specified as more or less healthy or by attending to the emotions which accompany the behaviors. Obviously the two are interrelated as inner and outer dimensions of the complete human action. The strategies are costly and ineffective because they do not relieve the unpleasant feelings, and in addition they create a sense of failure in the person using them.

Nowhere are the negative emotions more prominent than in instances where aggression and hostility are directed toward the self. Many people do not take care of themselves and mistreat themselves, but sometimes this lack of caring reaches pathological proportions. In some instances the other against whom hostility is actually intended is too threatening, and this may lead a person to turn the aggressive energies against himself. In most cases it is simply a matter of not liking or indeed even hating oneself. The reasons for this are many. In one person it may be because of some moral failure; in another because a life goal was never attained. Children sometimes butt their heads on the floor to get rid of hostile impulses, and older people who hate themselves accomplish the same results with not much more subtle forms of self-punishment.

All people from time to time take out their anger and aggressive feelings on themselves. Emotional affliction comes into the picture because of the degree and the persistence of such behavior. Sometimes the self-punishment is direct and obvious as in the case of persons who cut themselves or burn themselves. In most cases the self-directed aggression is better disguised and indirectly expressed.

We have already looked at the hypochrondriacal person who punishes himself with ulcers or headaches, and we have seen how often the part of the body which becomes impaired symbolizes the underlying emotional issue. A bad back may be a way of expressing anger about people who are always "on my back." A headache may reflect "feelings which I can't stand." In other cases the string of physical ailments becomes a way of mutilating, not any one organ, but part of one's whole life. Self-tormentors may complain bitterly about their pain and spend their energies and finances scurrying around from clinic to clinic trying to find relief. But visits to different doctors can easily distract from the real task of facing up to some conflict that generates the feelings of anger and aggression. Body punishment or self-directed hostility can be used as a management device for certain people. Bodily torment becomes a way of escaping from rather than facing up to upsetting situations and the threatening feelings which they generate. But self-hurting devices are costly and ineffective ways of adjusting.

The most prominent forms of self-hurting are alcoholism and drug abuse. Under the guise or relieving tension, or feeling good, the abuser of chemical substances turns large doses of anger and aggression against himself. Alcoholism and drug abuse, like other forms of self-punishment are instances of partial suicide or gradual self-destruction and as such qualify as second-level forms of emotional affliction.

What the common-sense viewer sees in alcohol and drug abuse is aggression and hostility directed toward the abuser's environment. The wives, parents, and children of these people come in for constant punishment. And so does society in the forms of insurance rates, accident victims, and lost productivity. But not quite so evident are the abuser's inner feelings and dread. Like the trout in our paradigm, the alcoholic makes exaggerated and futile gestures to relieve his sense of emotional turmoil. The chemicals used are types of self-medications for emotional pains and environmental upsets. The alcohol and drug abusers feel hooked, and the corresponding aggression gets turned against themselves. Each alcoholic binge, besides delivering a devastating blow to one's body, causes enormous hurt to others. After it's over intense guilt sets up the conditions for repeating the behaviors, which gradually become more and more obvious forms of self-mutilation.

The aggressive elements in alcoholism are also present in the adolescent who becomes frightened by the upcoming adjustment to adult life and takes refuge in abuse of other drugs. Rather than adopting economical and effective measures to handle the fears and conflicts which threaten emotional balance, some young people draw back. As we saw above with schizoid personalities, drugs become a form of relief from the fears of relationship and of the next stage of development. But like every other bad coping device, the behavior of drug abuse quickly creates even more serious problems than the ones it was orginally used to solve.

By forming social bonds of support and friendship with other drug abusers, young people build a sense of self and a set of meanings both of which are closely associated with drugs. If we look more closely at their lives we can also see the prominence of aggression and hostility. Hard rock or punk rock music which is a big part of the drug culture is full of anger and destructiveness. It is the self-hurting and the mutilizations of the self which young persons do not see and which they are most resistant to considering. The strong opposition they mount to any suggestion that self-destruction is part of their lifestyle is itself a strong indication of just that repressed awareness. Exaggerated opposition to news of health hazards from drug abuse is required to keep the self-hurting dimension of this coping strategy from surfacing. But it is just this self-punitive aspect of drug abuse that constitutes this behavior as an instance of emotional illness. A young person may grow out of it or may require professional help to develop healthier forms at coping.

Professional help should in some cases be considered because adolescents are in the process of forming their personalities, and once the patterns of drug abuse and self-destruction become ingrained they become very difficult to eradicate. Where drugs are used for disguised self-punishment, body tissues quickly become dependent on these substances and withdrawal creates painful problems. But even when things have not gone that far psychological dependency on the drug and its culture is developed which creates a different kind of withdrawal problem.

What we should not forget in our examination of forms of self-punishment and defects of caring is that the coping behaviors are initiated in order to respond to strong negative feelings which threaten emotional equilibrium. Self-destructive behaviors are expensive and ineffective strategies to control fear, anger, and overwhelming hostility. The bad strategies usually accomplish something, but they do so at too high a price, and they ignore other more effective coping devices. The first few times a person abuses alcohol or some other drug in order to seek relief from a sense of feeling hooked or terrified certainly do not qualify as an emotional problem. But as the practice continues, the problem becomes more serious.

Alcoholism and drug abuse can be looked at from any number of perspectives and will never be completely understood. From a psychiatric perspective, however, these ways of behaving are seen as defense mechanisms for bad feelings. If all the misery caused by chemical abuse were associated with some skin rash a national emergency would be declared and all the weapons of modern medicine would be mobilized to cure the problem. But emotional problems are not as obvious as a skin rash, and so we ignore them and laugh at them rather than see them for what they are.

Finally, one cannot mention self-directed aggression without referring to depression, which is even more widespread than alcohol and drug abuse. Depression is not necessarily part of the picture in cases of substance abuse but it figures in the picture so frequently that the psychiatrist is always on the lookout for its signs. Depression shares with substance abuse the structure of aggression-hostility turned against the self. It is a form of self-hurting and is so common that it can be found at any level of emotional upset. Depression at the second level is not so severe as to cause the total disability which characterizes fourth-level depression. Here it is a degree of not caring for oneself which takes the form of a lack of self-compassion. The self-hurting of second-level depression berates the self with thoughts of blame and failure which amount to a continual barrage of self-accusations. If we treated another person the way we sometimes threat ourselves we would rightfully be described as cruel, but we miss the cruelty in our attitude towards ourselves.

7. *Unusual strategies for managing aggression and hostilities—compulsions and sexual perversions*

Sometimes second-level emotional afflictions take the form of bizarre strategies for controlling the feelings of aggression and hostility.

Compulsions

Martha, a ten-year-old girl, had a particularly bad start in life. Her mother was a prostitute and had neither the time nor the disposition to provide much care for her baby. The child's most satisfying relationship was with a grandmother who became ill when she was six. During the next years the old woman's health deteriorated, and the child had to care for her during a long dying process. Martha interpreted the sad events of her life as instances of abandonment and uncaring behavior by others. Consequently she experienced all kinds of hostile and angry feelings toward her family. She often stated that she didn't care if everyone in her family died. Her hostile feelings were attached to frequent thoughts of death, which she controlled by compulsive actions. She would have to move her hand a certain way to keep people from dying. And she would ritualistically turn a light on and off a certain number of times to prevent death to certain people. Her compulsive actions were associated with obsessive thoughts which were full of aggression and hostility.

A compulsion is a repetitious act which someone feels compelled to make. The reasons for such actions are unconvincing even to the person doing them. And yet the actions are performed over and over. The real reasons are unconscious in the sense of being unknown to the performer and have to do with the control of threatening feelings. Compulsions that qualify as second-level emotional upsets are costly in that they seriously interfere with life and relationships. Obviously they are ineffective because they do not accomplish what they were intended to do.

Not-so-serious compulsions are found in many children who at some period feel compelled to touch every post on the way to school or step on (or over) every crack in the cement, or to walk on ledges and edges of the pavement, or to return home always on the same path. Some college students feel compelled to doodle during a lecture. These usually are the transitory compulsions which do not warrant professional attention. They are not costly, cause no pain, and do not interfere with life goals. But not all compulsions are of this benign sort.

A housewife I know developed a compulsion about cleaning. Washing and cleaning was not a reasonable response to dirt and disorder but rather a strategy for handling bad feelings. The behavior was costly, not only economically, but in a physical sense as well. Her skin was so inflamed by repeated exposures to harsh cleaning agents that she had to be hospitalized. Even before her skin got so bad she was either unable to go out or always late because of the cleaning compulsion. Here we see a good example of a costly and ineffective coping device. The underlying unconscious motivation for this activity was the control of aggression. Cleaning was her aggression-control ritual.

People today who are compulsive about certain exercises and dietary ritual are legion. Again, the underlying emotions are some variation of aggression and the behaviors are techniques of control. The compulsive control device may also accomplish an unconscious aggressive intention toward the self in the form of a severe self-punishment.

Dieting, for example, can become compulsive to the point that it qualifies as an emotional disturbance and so too can eating. Food lends itself easily to taking on added meaning. In fact it qualifies as one of the most powerful of human symbols. For one person it may symbolize love, for another filth, for a third material possessions. No matter what the meaning, food can be associated with compulsive acts of eating or messing or hoarding which at some point qualify as an emotional problem. Pathological compulsive actions are not only linked with aggression, but their repetitiousness pushes out truly effective action. As a result compulsive behavior is both costly and incapacitating.

Sexual Perversion

Although our age prides itself as being liberated from narrow puritanical limitations, there is still such a thing as sexual perversion, and it qualifies in this model of understanding as a form of emotional affliction.

Volumes have been written on perversion, and academic journals continue to pile up studies of every possible variation of sexual practice. Our attention to the subject does not presume to synthesize this mountain of information but rather to focus on one aspect of this behavior which often is overlooked or underplayed. Perversion provides a vehicle for the expression of strong hostile feelings more than is openly admitted and perverted sex contains large amounts of pain and hurt and self-destruction. Sadism is the most obvious example of this and serves as something of a paradigm for most perversion.

But there are advocates of sexual perversion who believe that any form of sexual behavior which people choose to engage in is automatically healthy. The tradition of the Marquis de Sade is not dead. Incest used to be considered the absolutely final line over which one could not step without qualifying as perverted, but recently incest has been referred to by ultimate sexual crusaders as the final obstacle to true sexual liberation. Even incest involving parents and young children is considered to be a subtle delight rather than a perversion by those who seek salvation through orgasm.

Most people have sense enough to recognize these practices

as both emotionally unhealthy and morally wrong, but there is no way of devising a schema for distinguishing health from illness in the area of sexuality which will gain universal agreement. However, if universal assent is a precondition for truth, there could be neither philosophy nor psychiatry. The line of reasoning here that places certain sexual practices outside the bounds of normality and emotional health focuses on the aggression and hostility in these behaviors. As with the other behaviors we have seen, emotional affliction is a matter of degree; and if the high level of aggressive feeling which underlies other types of problems is present in sexual behavior, so that it makes the act primarily destructive, then we have a case for calling it perversion rather than just an odd personal preference.

Any sexual behavior from which loving and caring are absent becomes suspect. Although there is a great latitude in the expression of sexual love, certain sexual forms pass beyond the broad range of normal behaviors either because of the source of sexual stimulation, or the type of sexual object, or the modality of its expression. Excess aggression and destructiveness is obvious in instances of rape and seduction of children. In other forms of perversion, aggression and destructive elements are not quite as obvious but nevertheless are there.

Normal sex is much broader than reproductive sex because it includes symbolic meanings beyond a literal biological understanding of the procreative function. But normal sex does not go beyond affection and care. There are aggressive elements in sexuality, and if there is doubt about this one need only notice how easily sexual terms become vehicles of aggression (Fuck you!). But healthy human sexuality cannot be dominated by aggressive feelings.

Some prefer to look at animal life to get a line on normality in human beings, but animal studies cannot bear the full weight of any line of reasoning about human sexuality. First, there is such variation in sub-human forms of sexuality that one has to begin such an approach by selecting what, according to a preconceived theory, constitutes significant animal behavior. Even after this is done nothing definite has been learned. Human beings are different. Sex in human beings has many levels of symbolic meaning which it never has in animals. There is individual variation within normal human sexuality, and some sublimated aggression, no doubt. But there are also standards of healthy sexual expression, and when these are violated we have crossed the line into the second level of emotional affliction.

The person, for example, who exposes himself to public humiliation and private disgrace by engaging in transitory homosexual acts in public toilets is engaging in potentially self-destructive behaviors. There is a self-directed hostility here just as there is other-directed hostility in the homosexual or the heterosexual behavior which involves constant seduction and abandonment of partners. Excessive aggression and hostility are present as well in all the lies and manipulations that constitute sexual seduction. The playboy trying to beat Don Juan's record as well as the homosexual leading a gay lifestyle are expressing more than high levels of sexual desire. They are expressing feelings of hate and hostility, both toward others and toward themselves. The high incidence of disease found among active indiscriminate homosexuals is both a symbol of the destructive components of their lifestyle and an effect of sexual perversion.

Acts like exposing oneself to children and other exhibitionistic and voyeuristic behaviors show the same dominant aggressive elements. They are vulgar, lewd, full of hostility, and they cause real hurt to others.

The gay liberation movement has turned the attitude of Andre Gide toward his homosexuality into a political movement. Like earlier liberation movements, gay liberation focuses on personal pride and political power. The movement has succeeded in breaking down some of the worst prejudices against homosexuals as well as some of the laws which unnecessarily restrict the homosexual's right to earn a living. But the thesis that homosexuality is a matter of personal taste, like the preference for chocolate rather than vanilla, slides over many of the unsavory and unhealthy aspects of homosexual practice: the degradation of sex partners, jealous rages, the exploitations, infecting and reinfecting self and others with all types of disease. The hostility and aggression which constitutes incest and sadism as perversion, permeates some homosexual practice and the gay lifestyle. The more unusual the sexual stimuli, the more unnatural the sexual objects, and the more bizarre the modalities of sexual expression, the more likely it is that sexual behavior will be dominated by excessive aggression and hostility.

All combined, perverted sexual practices constitute second-level types of emotional distress. In fact the perversion could serve as a paradigm of this level problem. The behaviors are costly. They involve tremendous suffering to self and others. Their ineffectiveness in providing real satisfaction is shown in the frequency of partner change and the compulsive repetitiousness of so much of the sexual activity. Finally, there is the use of sexuality as a vehicle for expressing hurt and hostility toward self and others. But the pervert is not crazy. He maintains contact with reality in most areas of life. He or she can function outside hospital settings, earn a living, and in some cases make considerable contributions to a chosen field.

8. A further deterioration of emotional health—
violent crime, battering, assault, rage: Level III

The strategies which we have been discussing as first- and second-level problems are not strange to any life. Every person comes under stress. Every self experiences overloads of negative feelings and adopts emergency devices like the ones we have been describing. Is there a person who has never worried too much, taken out aggression on the wrong one, hurt himself by drinking or overwork, fainted, harbored unfounded prejudice, suffered from an unreasonable fear, or had a curiosity at least about kinky sex? In most lives potentially pathological coping devices have at least occasionally been used. The fortunate among us adopt these stress-relieving devices only temporarily and manage with help from a friend or a change in the situation to work toward the normal range of behavior. It is only when these emergency devices become habitual, permanent, or integrated into a personality structure that we can speak of an emotional affliction.

If the emergency is such that the management strategies prove ineffective, then the situation may lead to the adoption of even more costly devices and consequently to even more serious forms of emotional turmoil. When the stresses do not recede and negative emotions continue to build, then sometimes the whole personality ruptures. There are situations which tax a human being beyond his limits. He may have stretched and compromised all he can. Or the effort to keep his balance through emergency devices may have worn down his resistance. In a weakened state and under an increased amount of emotional stress, the self may actually crack. Such occurrences take us to the next level of pathology.

The third-level emotional problem is defined as a rupture of the ego under emotional stress. The overstressed, overtaxed, overwearied self simply breaks up. The control function of the ego collapses and then the dangerous, destructive emotions explode. The outside usually receives the force of the explosion, but the destruction recoils in self-damage as well.

A sudden homicidal assault, for example, is an extreme example of ego rupture. Fits of rage are more common and less extreme forms. Criminal records are full of examples of these impulsively destructive acts. Occasionally the rage is directed against the self in mutilation or suicidal behaviors.

Crime is different in real life than it appears in novels. Many times the criminal really has no satisfactory explanation for his crime. A criminal behavior may result from an ego rupture which the criminal himself does not fully understand. In many cases the most important factors in terrible crime are unconscious emotions of hostility and rage.

Most people recognize the second-level coping devices we have discussed as instances of emotional distress. Not so however with third-level ruptures of the personality. In the popular mind these behaviors are frequently understood in legal rather than medical categories. They are understood as crime rather than afflictions.

In second-level forms of emotional disturbance, aggression is discharged in disguised and somewhat controlled form, but now control and disguise is lost. Certain criminal behaviors qualify as more serious forms of emotional affliction because in them the aggression which underlies all such problems becomes naked and extensive. In alcohol or drug abuse, e.g., family members are hurt, but in some criminal activity the aggression extends far beyond the family. It is both more direct and more destructive. The negative feelings reach such intensity that attempts to divert them are no longer successful.

What happens then is an overflowing of aggression on to the environment in the form of naked violence.

It has been only recently that this particular behavioral abnormality has been recognized as a form of serious emotional affliction. Child abuse, for example, which the psychiatrist has always been aware of, recently has been discovered by other groups, and attempts are being made to provide help for both the victims and the parents. The ego rupture which precedes such behaviors is recognized now as a form of emotional affliction that is better handled medically than in a strictly legal fashion. Assaults, too, lend themselves to analysis in emotional categories, and the following case will illustrate why they are sometimes classified as instances of emotional disorder.

An operator of large and powerful earth-moving equipment beat and badly battered his seven-year-old crippled son. Reading an account of the incident in the paper would cause generalized disbelief and deep-seated revulsion against the perpetrator of such a hideous crime. Learning more about the case shows that it was not just a crime, but also an instance of emotional breakdown.

The father operated gigantic equipment. He was however a small and twisted runt of a man who was tormented and ridiculed by his fellow workers. The work exhausted him, and he drank for relief of his many problems. He had a very unsatisfying relationship with his wife who tormented him at home by making fun of his inadequacies. She disliked the son, and when a schoolteacher advised that he be taken out of school because he was feeebleminded, she laughed and compared the boy to his father. In response the father tried to help his son with his school work. He stopped drinking and threw himself into this added task with its own peculiar stresses and new pressures. On the evening in which the beating occurred, he was physically exhausted but started in to try to teach the boy to count to twenty. The boy could get as high as thirteen but then got mixed up and could go no further. The wife, who was listening to everything, laughed and gave him the "I told you so" look. At that moment he exploded. The boy was screaming out numbers at random while the father administered a violent beating. "I blew up," he said, and, "I beat him. The next thing I remember was the neighbor screaming." People on the street said the father had gone crazy, and they were right.

Like other forms of emotional affliction, attacks of rage can be treated. The man in this case, in fact, with professional help was able to strengthen his controls, reorder his life patterns, and nurture the son who never lost affection for his father.

Direct and uncontrolled hostility is the external shape of this level of illness. Internally it shows up as a complete but temporary breakdown in the person's powers of self-control. Later on, the act of violence may be rationalized as self-defense, or getting back, or even giving in to a pleasurable impulse. At the time of the violent act, however, what takes place is a breakdown of the human personality, and although the person may recover later on and act in a perfectly normal way, every such breakdown, like a blowout on a tire, weakens the personality structure and makes it vulnerable to another such occurrence.

Although naked violence is not ordinarily thought of as a type of emotional breakdown, common language descriptions of it carry some awareness of this aspect of the problem. People talk of a violent person "losing it," "going berserk," "coming unglued," "losing his head," "going crazy," "going to pieces."

Violence does involve a temporary emotional breakdown,

and anyone unfortunate enough to have been in the presence of naked aggression knows that it is a form of craziness. Pop psychologies, under the neutral banner of assertiveness, teach people to be aggressive, but no reasonable person endorses naked aggression. Only television programmers believe that bold public scenes of mad slaughtering and overt destructiveness are forms of manly behavior and even beneficial for children to watch.

From a psychiatric perspective, however, rather than being an idealized test of real manliness, naked aggression is a breakdown of necessary emotional restraint. It represents an even more radical movement away from reality than what we examined as second-level behaviors. Now the behavior is not a costly way of keeping one's balance in a threatening or upsetting environment but a temporary, complete loss of balance. It is the temporary character of this device that makes it appealing to some as a way of releasing destructive impulses which threaten to overwhelm them. Third-level coping devices, like all the rest, are ways of managing bad feelings, and like the rest they are costly and ineffective.

The sequence of events leading up to this level of disorder may be something like the following. An offense of some kind takes place or is imagined. Feelings of aggression and hostility are engendered and intensified over time until they disturb the person's reality-testing ability. He becomes entangled in a world of injuries and resentments which create an unbearable inner tension and keep him from thinking through the consequences of his actions. Mocking or some form of humiliation takes place, a real or imagined provocation, and what follows is an explosion of violence.

Sometimes the sufferer is aware of an impending explosion. One very slight middle-aged man came to the emergency ward of a city hospital and told the physician that he was afraid he was going to kill someone. The young doctor was just uncomfortable enough in his presence to call for help from the police. When they arrived, it took six men, each twice his size, to keep him under control. Once the situation was such that he could let himself go, an explosion of murderous rage occurred. The all-important controls gave way under the pressure of destructive emotion.

The explosion associated with this level's problem is one of major proportion. The buildup of emotional pressure can be tremendous, and when the rupture occurs enormous damage is done both to the environment and to the self. We usually focus on the outside damage: the person or persons who were assaulted, the property which was destroyed. But the person who explodes also suffers. Temporarily there may be a feeling of relief, but following the release the self is weakened and when upsets cause the same emotions to build, the same thing is likely to happen.

Most people know what it is like to be on the point of exploding with murderous aggression. Parents are often pushed to this point by children, especially older children. And anyone who has ever lost control knows the sense of disorganization which precedes it, the costliness of the destructive behavior, and the humiliation associated with impairment of perception and judgment. If you have blown up on an occasion, you know how much like a crazy person you become. More than likely you retained some control and judgment so that the damage was kept in check. Now imagine the case where all control is lost, and you can see why this behavior qualifies as a form of emotional affliction. The blind, destructive lashing out on the part of someone with enormous pools of hatred and hostility makes news under the banner of crime, but it can just as easily be described as an instance of serious emotional breakdown. In some cases the blowout is a onetime brush with serious emotional illness, and in other cases the personality ruptures time and again. There are personalities which are more like battlegrounds than anything else, and continuing conflicts going on within create such aggressive feelings that almost anything can trigger a destructive release. As with other forms of emotional disturbance, the eruptions function as ways of forestalling an even more serious problem. In effect, these temporary disorders are a way of avoiding more permanent breakdowns.

Many criminals act like little children who blow up all the time and hit out at everyone and everything around them. Others do the kind of violence that we may have harbored in our hearts only once and managed later on with help from others to overcome. The person who chronically loses control of aggressive feelings, however, has a serious problem. He spends his life causing misery and pain to himself and to others. When he is not expressing overt and naked aggression, he is stealing, which is aggression only very slightly disguised. The popular term "to rip off" shows the hostile and destructive dimension of taking something of worth away from someone.

Repeated explosions of aggression and hostility are frequently associated with a cluster of other characteristics which join to constitute the classification of psychopath or antisocial personality: defiance, superficial relationships, absence of concern for others, deceitfulness, lack of remorse and conscience. This particular personality disorder is more serious than others; more aggressive, more destructive, and more difficult to change. This type personality is only a short step from the full-blown emotional disorder called psychosis to which we now turn. Before making the turn however, let me make a disclaimer. In calling criminal assaults like batterings and even murder a form of emotional breakdown, I do not mean to reduce a complex human action to just this one dimension, but rather to call attention to the psychiatric dimension that is frequently overlooked in criminal behavior.

9. *Full-blown emotional breakdowns—depression, mania, schizophrenia, paranoia: Level IV*

When negative emotions are overwhelming and beyond the capacity of lower-level coping devices to contain, then the progessive process of worsening emotional health takes a giant step into illness. Before this point is reached, less pathological regulation devices have usually failed. The wholesale explosions we just discussed may have occurred with increasing frequency without bringing about a healthy balance. Temporary relief may have been followed by more complications, increased tension, and even weaker capacities to cope. And so the move is made to even more drastic emergency measures which constitute what most people understand as emotional illness. In psychosis or insanity we reach the extremes of personality disorganization and the most bizarre of all the emergency gestures. In each case this state is preceded by intense, negative feelings and a sense that one's very life is in danger. At this stage the emotional distress is beyond the ability of laymen to handle. It qualifies the sufferer for full patient status and brings him or her into contact with the psychiatric professional.

Readers may not have been aware that the stages leading to what is generally understood to be emotional illness are themselves lower levels of illness. The lesser forms of dysfunction and lower levels of emotional affliction are usually called eccentricity, or viciousness, or queer behavior rather than illness, and those who suffer from them may neither have been given patient status nor come into contact with mental health professionals. Traditionally, emotional illness has been a term for the end states and most extreme levels of dysfunction. The person who qualified as emotionally ill was thought of as having an "unusual disease" which separated him from the rest of us. What we have tried to show is that just the opposite is actually the case: that the extreme forms are related to the lower-level behaviors and one can make sense of emotional afflictions by seeing them as a set of progressively more costly and ineffective techniques for avoiding disintegration of the self in the face of intense negative feelings.

Our goal has been to provide for the layman a way of making sense out of the topic of emotional distress, but more importantly to make it possible for anyone to survey his own behavior and identify his own unhealthy coping devices. Knowing that a particular behavior is costly and ineffective may be all that is needed to initiate change. Understanding is the beginning of therapy.

Our basic metaphor for understanding this complex thing that happens to human beings has been that of a hooked fish. We all swim around making certain moves to gain satisfaction, self-esteem, and positive feeling states. Then changes occur which disturb our routines. The smooth flow of emotional life becomes disturbed, and we make emergency movements to handle the new situation (first-level coping devices). In some cases these succeed. In other cases the situation itself changes, positive feelings return, and we are relieved.

But there are times when the emergency measures fail and more extreme behaviors are employed to cope in the sense of keeping one's balance (second-level devices). Sometimes these succeed in establishing a costly adjustment and become permanent parts of a personality structure. In psychiatry, these are referred to as neurotic personalities.

But there are instances in which even neurotic devices fail. Then a rupture or blowout may occur under pressure (third-level coping devices). Such explosions may take place frequently, thereby creating increased stress from the environment and even more negative feelings within the weakened self. If the personality ruptures are minor in intensity (a temper tantrum, a spree of some kind), they may relieve the pressure and permit the person to resume normal functioning.

But if satisfaction and significance become more and more difficult to realize as a result of their employment, or if even more intense negative feelings move in to dominate every waking moment, then the only way left to salvage some semblance of life is illness (fourth-level coping devices). Emotional illness is for the sufferer an alternative to death: the only way to keep some semblance of existence in a world of impending doom.

To some extent each of us wears a mask of sanity. Underneath or deep within each person lie emotions which can bring about personality disintegration. No one is perfectly safe or so healthy that emotional deterioration could not take place. We are all vulnerable. The face we show to the world is not our whole self. As anyone who marries soon finds out, there are other aspects of him or her, unsavory and somewhat unstable, which the stress of intimacy brings to the surface and which the spouse confirms and criticizes. Occasionally the face we show publicly and in superficial relations conceals a considerable undercurrent of anger, bitterness, and hostility. If these negative emotions are sufficiently intense, they can threaten job, marriage, and even health. Explosive forces beneath the surface can sometimes cause cracks even in a social facade. Some people show degrees of illness in public under the influence of disinhibiting drugs like alcohol and marijuana. Sometimes the whole thing falls apart and the face of insanity appears.

Once self-control or the coping mechanisms collapse, hostile negative feelings flood the person and inform his behavior. When a full-blown nervous breakdown occurs, it includes a repudiation of what we call reality, and all kinds of distortions both of self and outside world. Emotions become exaggerated, thoughts confused, behavior unpredictable, and productivity disappears completely. No wonder ancient people thought a demon had taken possession of the person. In outward appearance a frightening shift takes place. The characteristics we expect from human beings suddenly disappear and the demonic makes its appearance.

And yet even in bizarre and chaotic behavior the psychiatrist can discover patterns and meanings. Threads and fragments can be pieced together to get a line on the inner feelings which are causing the personality disorganization. The world in which a person lives may have become too threatening, and within the self there are no coping devices adequate to terrible and threatening feelings. It may be a fear of being alone or unloved that is too much to handle. It may be some form of death that causes too much fear for a weak personality structure to endure. Early childhood may have left the person with radical feelings of insecurities and pools of unresolved hostility which rob him or her of hope. Once a good psychiatrist puts his finger on the underlying feelings he can begin to help the person find less costly and more effective ways of coping. Even people in the fourth level of emotional illness get better.

What do fourth level behaviors look like? They are not beautiful but are fairly well-known. Even the names which are used today to describe them go back thousands of years.

Melancholia or Depression

Why put depression at the fourth level of emotion affliction? Doesn't everyone get depressed from time to time? Yes, certainly, and yet there are depressions that are so severe as to qualify with the serious forms of emotional illness. Severe depression in fact is one of the few types of emotional disorder which causes death.

The trouble with understanding depression is that we have only one word for both symptom and the underlying disease. Sometimes the symptoms are minor and may indicate nothing more than a realistic response to some bad luck. But in other cases the symptoms are grave and reflect a serious underlying emotional disorder which requires immediate professional attention. We could have talked about depressions at every level because they appear in every degree of seriousness. What we focus on here are the most serious levels, in light of which we can better understand the more benign forms.

Everyone knows what depression is like. Depression moves along the scale of increasing severity as the characteristic behaviors become more costly, ineffective, and incapacitating. These are easily recognized: a physical slowing down which includes a stooped body position, sagging face, dropped head; loss of appetite and constipation; and finally sleep disturbances, usually in the form of early morning awakenings. Behind these are the negative feelings: the pervasive feelings of sadness; feeling worthless, incompetent and inadequate; feeling guilty and angry at oneself.

On the face of it depression looks like the very opposite of the aggressive and hostile feelings which we have argued are at the root of all forms of emotional affliction. The depressed person looks like a whipped puppy dog rather than an angry Doberman. But appearances are deceiving. The aggressive component in depression in fact is comparable to what we find in dangerous criminals. Indeed, there is assault and destruction being carried out, but it is against the self rather than against others. In all degrees of severity, emotional illness is costly to the self, but in full-blown depression the whole thrust of aggression and hostility is turned directly on the self. Depression, at least in its serious, clinical forms, is self-assault and self-punishment, comparable in severity to the worst physical child-beating, wife-beating, raping, stealing, murdering, and the like, but it is just as destructive to the person against whom it is aimed.

Serious depression is in fact a type of self-murdering or progressive suicide. There are of course degrees of severity, but at the extreme angry, hostile feelings cause a disorganization of the self and a loss of contact with reality. The criminal disregards the social consequences of his behavior and the depressed person is just as unrealistic in his negative thinking and self-judgments. In both cases there are intense feelings of aggression being discharged, a loss of common sense, lack of reasonable vision of the past, present and future, and almost insurmountable resistance to help. The only way to get any sicker is to take physical steps to destroy oneself.

Because depression is a stranger to no one, there is little need for clinical examples of the disorder. We need only look at some particularly bad time in our lives to recall what depression is like. What we may not know about depression is that it strikes even the young. A separation from the mother can cause even a baby or a young child to become depressed.

Unless something is done, within weeks the baby stops protesting, gives up, and does not even respond to the mother when she appears; finally the baby dies. Depression in fact can strike at any age. The breakup of a marriage and the separation of children from one another or from one of the parents can trigger depression, which may appear as sadness. The child who withdraws and becomes very shy and generally sick may be depressed.

College students frequently get so depressed that they are forced to leave school. One of my students last semester started out in high spirits and involved in all kinds of activities. She joined a sorority, had a steady boyfriend, and was making excellent grades. Then she broke up with the boyfriend and shortly after that her mother died. When she returned to school after the funeral, she could not study and had trouble sleeping. She skipped class often and the farther back she fell in her work, the worse she felt about herself and the more she was unable to get back to her studies. At night she would feel a little better and resolve to get going but by morning she felt so low that getting out of bed was a task. The thought of failed courses and parental disappointment caused intense feelings of guilt and shame. Finally she required hospitalization.

The story ended well. She followed advice and stayed out of school for a semester. This gave her time to grieve. She cried a lot, talked a lot, and gradually began to put things together. When the next semester rolled around she was ready to be productive again. I saw her yesterday and she looked fine.

Depression, then, is widespread and not confined to any age. The elderly frequently get depressed, and so do people during middle age. Even newlyweds and people who have just gotten good news fall into depression. There is usually a loss of some sort involved, and the loss can be physical (a sickness), psychological (a relationship), financial, or whatever. Loss is difficult for anyone, but some seem less able to bear it than others. It generates the hostile feelings which, turned against oneself, produce this potentially serious and very common form of illness. Depression actually occurs at many different intensities and could be listed at any one of the previous levels. The depressive feelings at the fourth level are so deep that they threaten a person's survival and may even cause a cognitive defect which intensifies the person's detachment from reality.

Mania (Frenzy)

Mania looks like the very opposite of depression and many persons who suffer from mood depressions which go far below normal also suffer from mood elevations that go far above it. If depression is feeling too sad, mania is feeling too happy, but both terms are inadequate to describe what actually goes on in these disorders. Everything is speeded up in mania, including speech and physical activity. In fact, the manic person is characterized by almost continuous motion accompanied by elation and excitement. The manic person feels on top of things, takes on enormous projects, and pursues unrealistic goals with seemingly unlimited energy.

But how can mania be classified as a fourth-level disorder? How can it be understood as a progessively more severe aggression and destructiveness? It would seem to be just the opposite. The manic person is hyperalert and hyperactive. He is in high spirits and going at a speedway pace: sleeping too little, talking too much, reacting to everything, and seemingly incapable of fatigue. The manic does not even take time to eat. His coping devices, like those of the passive-aggressive personality, have the knack of driving everyone around him crazy.

At just this point we begin to see the aggressive underside of this unhealthy coping device. The activity of the manic person is a way of releasing aggression, and those unfortunate enough to be associated with him feel the full impact. Even when activity is laced with humor, the hostility is there. Everyone and everything in the environment is consumed or devoured. Considerable amounts of hostility are discharged in an attempt to release emotional pressure and keep from getting even worse. Like depression, mania is a flight from reality and a denial of the way things really are. Positive emotions are used to deny threatening ones or to flee from involvement with an unpleasant reality.

Like depression, mania comes in degrees of severity. What we are describing under fourth-level disorders is extreme. In less severe forms all the symptoms are present, but in a weaker form. There is a separate psychiatric category called hypomania or low mania which is sometimes difficult to distinguish from a driving and intense personality. Understandably, it is difficult to intervene in such a situation, because this form of emotional disorder is characterized by intensely positive feelings, indeed a kind of ecstasy. The problem is comparable to persuading persons with high blood pressure to take medicine when they feel terrific. High feels better than normal, but it has distinctly destructive features.

I know a physician who sees twice as many patients as anyone else. He is able to get up during the night on a case and still go full-speed the next day. It is his habit to do two or three things at the same time. He is a living dynamo.

An investment consultant and insurance broker with whom I do a little business is the same type person. He seems to have unlimited enthusiasm. Every conceivable type of investment he knows about and can talk about with great conviction. Besides his nonstop business activity (he always stops by my house at night on his way to someone else) he is the chairman of the heart fund, on the board of the YMCA, and a competitive runner.

These high-energy types border on mania, and sometimes there is an event in their lives that kicks them over the line. It is questionable whether they use good judgment in conducting their lives, but once the line is crossed the question is removed. Really bad judgment joined to intense and exhausting activity signals the beginning of the fourth-level degree of this emotional illness. The blowups which characterize third-level illness last only a short while but manic phases of an emotional disorder can go on for a long time. The resulting destruction can be enormous.

Schizophrenia

This is a very general term which literally means a split in the personality.The sufferer becomes split off from the real world, from other people, and even from parts of his very self. The schizophrenic can become totally absorbed in himself, and in some cases regress to early infancy when as a baby he was the whole world. In addition, schizophrenia is characterized by bizarre behaviors, incoherent speech, delusional ideas, and an indifference to manners and social expectations. The activity of the schizophrenic becomes robot-like, except for occasional sudden outbursts.

People who suffer from schizophrenia usually start out with an emotional problem that goes back to earliest childhood. The bonds with reality that are broken in this fourth-level disorder were already thin and frail because of early deprivation and too many negative feelings. Then come the stresses and pressures of later life, and a weakened ego, or one that is exhausted by the use of less severe but ineffective management devices, becomes overtaxed and breaks. Then, the reality which stresses and pressures the person is simply withdrawn from.

But how is this aggressive? In the sense that schizophrenia destroys both outside reality and the reality-testing capacities within the self. Loyalty to reality is denounced, including the reality of friends and loved ones.

The ordinary person has little contact with fourth-level types of emotional distress, and there is no disagreement among those who treat such patients about the severity of this disorder. Since our goal in this book is to provide a model for understanding emotional affliction which can aid the non-professional in examining and managing his or her life, there is no reason for extensive examination of these extreme forms of illness. Caring for persons suffering from illness in this intensity is the responsibility of a psychiatrist.

But we do need to see how these classical problems fit into the model being discussed. How are they to be understood as more severe instances of the behaviors we have already examined? Feelings of threat, fear, terror, guilt, and despair are triggered off by feeling hooked in a situation which does not seem open to change. In turn, these negative emotions and persistently upsetting external conditions increase tension to the breaking point. Dangerous aggressive impulses are thereby aroused which in turn increase the threat and terror. Potential disorganization then is controlled by radical regulatory devices: the withdrawal from reality, the absorption into fantasy, concentration on the self alone. These coping mechanisms both control aggressive feelings and are manifestations of aggression (e.g., the destruction of reality). So, cut off from reality, the psyche of the person is dominated by

dreamlike products of his own unconscious mind. He be-
haves like someone acting out a crazy dream.

How can this process be justified as a regulatory device to
serve adjustment and balance? The fourth-level regulatory
devices are self-destructive, but on the other hand, they are
also self-preserving. They are meant to avert more complete
destruction. These devices establish some emotional equilibrium by retreating from the threat. As regulatory devices and
defense mechanisms become more extreme, the cost to the
self for their use increases. In fourth-level disorders, the self
is saved from death but at the cost of being estranged from
reality and absorbed in fantasies. Insanity is a substitute for
death.

Military hospitals have many patients for whom the war
created just such overtaxing stressful situations. Many young
men cracked up under the abnormal pressures of battle.
Many recovered once they returned to a more normal and less
threatening environment. But some never did.

In other cases it is business, or school, or relationships, or
storms, or bankruptcy which cause the break. Unusual situations strain the powers of adjustment and the breakdown
takes as many forms as there are personalities.

One very rich young lady had been raised in the lap of lux-
ury and had been weakened by a lack of exposure to difficulties of any sort. Once arrived at college, the difficulties
came first in the form of classes she felt unable to manage.
While under great stress from the school situation she got
herself involved in an explosive sexual affair with one of her
professors. Not only was the teacher hotheaded, but so were
his wife and their four children. The affair became public and
was accompanied by public scenes and threatening harass-
ments. Suddenly, the girl began to hear voices which told her
all sorts of things about the wife, the professor, and the

children. She began to write letters to people on campus about her babies (she had none), talking about their running loose in the city without care. She had fantasies of being a queen and a powerful figure in the Mafia. Sometimes she was stiff and straight and over-polite. At other times she would explode and break up everything around her. She always talked about the Mafia and what they were going to do to her enemies. Obviously she had abandoned a threatening reality in favor of a world in which she had powerful allies and some control. All the talk of Mafia reflected her intense hostility which was generated by an uncontrolled and chaotic life situation. No one needs help in recognizing emotional illness here. The girl had become seriously ill and her illness consisted of the use of very costly coping devices for maintaining some control over her threatening and tumultuous emotions.

Paranoia

The victims of a psychotic break sometimes substitute a wonderful fantasized existence for real life and appear to be happy in their new creation. But more frequently the underlying aggression and hostility are only weakly restrained by the insanity. This is particularly true of paranoid illness which is characterized by preoccupations with persecution. The persecutors are usually very powerful and the fact that they have such intense interest in the patient enhances his sense of importance. On the surface the paranoid person may not seem as disturbed as the schizophrenic. In fact he may be very convincing in the way he has worked out the details of a wide-ranging plot against him. But the paranoid person feels hooked, is afraid of coming unstuck, and consequently is full of agggression, and as such is dangerous.

Assassins are often paranoid. So are the people who hole

up in a tower or on a roof and shoot people indiscriminately. Once the paranoid person moves away from reality in favor of a world of his own design no amount of reasoning or evidence or contrary testimony will make much difference. Everything that happens is fit into the insane scheme of things, which connects all kinds of separate events to plots of persecution and revenge.

A farmer who belonged to an evangelical sect and read a lot of his church's anti-Catholic tracts began to talk of being spied on by the local Catholic priest. The priest, he believed, had wired his farm with all kinds of listening devices and kept constant watch on his whereabouts. Conversations had to be held out in the field to avoid eavesdropping, and even then there was no assurance of privacy. At the same time he began to suspect his wife of having affairs with everyone in town. Anytime she went to the store or anyone came to the house, it was interperted as part of a system of contacts and associated with sexual activity. Finally he tied her in with the priest and the spy system. Ordinarily the farmer stayed to himself and spoke very little, but once he got excited he would spend hours trying to convince his wife both of the Catholic plot and her own infidelities. He did a number of hateful things to her, and finally got a gun with which he threatened to kill her unless she confessed.

Outside the family no one knew anything about this very dangerous form of emotional illness because the farmer, who had always been considered a little strange, did not appear publicly to have changed in any way. His business was carried on as usual, and he handled his church responsibilites with great care. The wife finally went to the police who had him committed temporarily. His blood relatives were incensed by this, got a lawyer, and secured his release. One week later, he killed his wife and shot a number of people who came to the house before being captured and rehospitalized.

The underlying aggression in this particular variation of fourth-level illness cannot be missed. The bizarre behavior both expresses feelings of hostility and attempts ineffectively to control them. Hatred, anger, and hostility reach unbearable intensities and are projected on others who then become a threatening enemy. As these negative emotions increase in intensity, the patient adopts more and more costly coping devices which in turn represent more and more serious forms of illness.

Minor emotional upsets are usually handled by almost everyone with healthy or only slightly dysfunctional devices. But as the emotions increase in intensity, more and more extreme mechanisms are called for. It is everyone's task and challenge to keep his emotional balance or maintain a degree of adjustment in the face of change. But as internal and external events make adjustment difficult, the use of the temporary coping devices are called for which have been the focus of our discussion. Arranging these according to levels of greater costliness and ineffectiveness, we arrive at one way of understanding the awful complexity which goes by the general term of emotional disorders.

If, however, emotional distress is not some rare disease but rather a combination of intense negative feelings and incapacitating defense mechanisms, then we have to conclude that we are all possible victims. In order to avoid the most severe manifestations of emotional affliction, we need to recognize which of our coping behaviors are healthy and which are potentially incapacitating. Recognition and understanding is the crucial first step in improving emotional health and facilitating adjustment.

One need not be a professional to understand the basic principles of emotional health and illness. And helping oneself is ordinarily a realistic goal. The final section of this book will focus on therapy in the sense of self-help, a therapy which will be based on recognition and better understanding of our feelings and the devices we customarily use to handle them. But first, to bring our model to completion, we have to look at a fifth and final level of emotional illness which can be understood as the triumph of aggressive and hostile feelings.

10. Suicide, the ultimate in flawed coping devices: Level V

All the strategies and devices which characterize emotional problems are failures of a sort. Usually, however, the failures are not fatal. In fact, most people who become emotionally upset, in the absence of degenerating conditions in the nervous system, do recover. Either the stressful situation which led to the adoption of exaggerated strategies changes, or the person achieves a better emotional balance with the aid of medication and insight therapy. But there are refractory cases which are resistant to every attempt to help. These become the chronic emotional disorders. Instead of getting better, some people who start out at lower levels of disorganization, get progressively worse. The ultimate failure, however, is death itself. The most costly and most ineffective of all coping devices is suicide.

There are many different forms of suicide, and each case, no matter how simple it may appear to be, is more complex than any interpretation that might be offered to explain it. There are as many perspectives that can be taken on suicide as there are perspectives on the human condition generally:

physical, neuro-chemical, social, ethical, religious, philo-sophical, and psychiatric. Our perspective sees suicide either as an instance of emotional illness or as an ever-present danger associated with it.[2] The tragedy of suicide is that it is a death which may have been avoided. The victims of suicide in psychiatric settings are in fact often people who show signs of improvement or are actually on the way to recovery. More-over, the suicide victim is frequently a person with excep-tional talent and high potential for contributing to society. (Suicide rates are particularly high among professional per-sons with good educations.)

The perspective taken in this book is that suicide is a very bad device which certain persons choose in order to cope with unbearable feelings. If emotional illness is characterized by expensive and ineffective devices for handling negative feel-ings, then suicide is the most costly and least efficient of these devices. It is adopted as a way of coping or as a way out of a particularly unhappy situation. Like all the other forms of emotional disorder there is in suicide a strong element of ag-gression and hostility. Some take out their hostile urges in death-dealing behaviors like drug addiction which are slowly self-destructive. Others take the quicker and more direct route.

If psychiatric models provide a perspective on suicide, it is not the "common sense" explanation one usually hears from friends of the deceased or the perspective one gets from newspaper accounts of this tragic occurrence. Financial troubles, the failure of a love relationship, grief over a spouse, all of these are commonly cited as causes of suicide. They are, however, more accurately understood as upsetting, but alone they are not sufficient to cause a suicide. Suicide, like other forms of emotional illness, is a device used to cope with intense negative feelings. Suicide is a final emergency device resorted to after others have been tried and have failed.

The sad thing is that too few people recognize the pre-suicidal gestures, or, if recognized, they are not taken seriously. For example, people who are depressed for a long time inevitably think about suicide. After suffering for a long time, death can begin to look sweet. Suicide may be talked about, and all such talk should be taken seriously. If the talk includes a plan of action (e.g., how it will be done, when, etc.), then professional help should be summoned.

But depression is not the only pre-suicidal behavior. Any number of other coping devices may have been tried and found ineffective. Only then the distressed and disorganized person moves to the ultimate in flawed management strategy. High incidence of suicide follows the failure of alcohol, sexual perversion, crime, and other costly strategies to manage painful negative feelings. When a case of suicide is closely examined, one can usually find evidence of other flawed coping behavior preceding the final act of self-destruction.

Suicide has this in common with other forms of emotional disorders: the person feels hooked and responds with feelings of rage, hatred, and hostility to the frustration. Because reality is considered too painful to be dealt with rationally, flight from reality becomes the preferred "solution." In one act, the suicide strikes an angry blow against himself and at the same time against another person or the situation which created his emotional upheaval. The hurt which is delivered to others (doctors, lovers, family) cannot be overlooked in trying to understand suicide. Revenge of a very childish sort plays an important part in many suicides. In this most severe degree of emotional illness, aggression and hostility overflow all restraints and do their deadly destructive thing.

Suicide in this admittedly limited perspective is the most severe of all forms of illness, and yet even at this level it shows traces of continuity with what we usually talk about as normal coping mechanisms. Many people, for example, commit suicide in fantasy. Their dreams are full of being hanged, executed, or killed in some way. There are feelings of self-hatred and exaggerated guilt in many lives which do not lead to actual suicide but which generate nocturnal suicides in the form of self-punishing and self-destructive dreams.

And then, too, there are accidental suicides. There are people who do not actually intend to commit suicide, but only to make a very strong statement about a need for help or sympathy or whatever: the person, for example, who takes an overdose of pills and then calls his doctor, or his wife, or the ambulance. But if the numbers are busy or too much traffic detains the help, suicide takes place by accident. There are, also, many suicides which are fully intended and successfully carried out but appear publicly to be accidents. Many a fatal car crash is an "accidentally on purpose" suicide. Even death from disease or in some cases spontaneous death can be brought on by the wish to kill oneself or to be killed.

Suicide is always complex, and each individual suicide adds its peculiar twists. For some it is a way of escaping, a flight from pain or feelings of persecution or the fear of becoming dependent. As such it is frequently accompanied by a fantasy of continued existence. It may just as likely be an exaggerated form of communication or a way of becoming a sacrificial hero to some cause. ("See how I have suffered," or "See what I had to do.") Often it is an act of revenge, a way of hurting those who remain. The suicide takes delight in the thought of remorse he will cause in those who rejected him (revenge is sweet). Finally, suicide may be a way killing, a murdering of a hated world or an unfaithful lover or a resented parent. The unforgettable mass suicide in Jonestown probably had something of each of these motivations. And most people will recognize that these suicides are evidence of advanced forms of illness.

Each of the five levels of emotional disorder we have looked at tells us something about the human condition. The human being distinguishes himself from other animals as much by the adoption of bizarre symbolic behaviors of adaptation as he does by his capacity for speech, free choice, reflection, science, art, or religion. Like other animals, man has aggressive and hostile feelings, but no other animal demonstrates the variety of symbolic expression of these emotions and only man turns them against himself. All the different forms of emotional affliction have been looked at as instances of aggression directed against the self, either crudely or in some indirect form. All forms then turn out to be modified versions of suicide.

If even the lesser forms of emotional problems contain aggressive and self-destructive elements, it is not surprising that there is so much suicide among the emotionally ill. Depression is hostile and aggressive no less than sadism and psychosomatic disorders. Aggressive thoughts and suicidal impulses are part of the picture of emotional illness. They show up even in a high incidence of suicide among those who care for disturbed people.

Calling attention to this dimension of emotional illness does not purport to be a total explanation. There are as many important perspectives on this complex mystery as there are dimensions of man. And each era devises a new model to try to pull together the many perspectives only to realize that the human condition generally, or even an individual human person, is too complex for man's model-building capacity. How, for example, does one find a model to understand the patterns of connectedness among the billions of brain cells when the sheer number of elements, let alone the intricacies of communication, are beyond the capacity of the world's largest computers? And what is so privileged about using computer circuitry as a model of understanding? Did God create according to our era's technological devices? It is certain that there will be something to replace the computer and that this new technology will make computer analogies to the human condition obsolete. We have to struggle to understand but at the same time be resigned to the limitations of our understanding.

In this book we are focusing on coping devices to gain emotional balance and on the place of aggressive and destructive feelings in emotional illness. The merit of this approach is its simplicity. We did not attempt to trace the origins of each emotional disorder or to delve into the mysteries of brain physiology or neurochemistry. But in choosing to focus on negative feelings and coping devices we call attention to what in dynamic psychiatry is considered a central issue.

Boiled down to its simplest formulation, human existence is a struggle between life and death forces. The life forces are called creativity, love, significance, power. The names of death forces are rage, hatred, revenge, aggression, hostility. These latter are stimulated by frustration or deprivation, and they are associated with stressful environments. Unless held in check, the death forces can overwhelm a person. They lead to the adoption of bizarre coping devices or striking departures from ordinary behavior patterns which are what we mean by emotional afflictions. Unpronounceable Greek names are used to specify the problems, and incomprehensible theories are formulated to explain their development. Our project in this book has been to call attention to elements of hostility and to see emotional disorder as a process which moves from ordinary coping devices to the most destructive and ineffective ones.

Now that we have in place a simple vision, we can turn to think about our own lives. We can examine some of our common feeling experiences and look at some of our common coping strategies for managing them.

III. COPING WITH PAINFUL FEELINGS

1. Thinking and Talking about Feelings

The emphasis in this final section is on treatment but not the professional sort which takes place in a psychiatrist's office or mental hospital. This book is directed to people who have to struggle with all the conflicts and upsets which can lead to mental illness but who lack the resources for getting professional help. Only a small percentage of Americans ever see a psychiatrist, and yet most everyone experiences periods of upset and turmoil which may cause a transitory form of illness. These people need help and in most cases either have to help themselves or depend upon a friend to get them over a rough period.

Just knowing how the more serious types of emotional illness come about can be of help. And understanding just a bit about the unpleasant and unhappy feelings generated by life's unavoidable conflicts and upsets may be all that is needed at some point to keep a person from adopting the worst sort of coping device. The therapy we will focus on in the final section then is self-therapy.

There is a saying that only a fool hires himself as his lawyer, and the same standard wisdom applies to a person in serious mental trouble. Once mental illness moves beyond temporary bad coping behavior into more set forms of ineffective adjustment, then professional help is required to move back within normal ranges. But before these serious stages are reached a person who understands his feelings a little better can move away from some of the most costly regulatory devices for handling them. People do set themselves down and have a talk with themselves about alternatives to their feelings, attitudes and reactions. There is such a thing as self-help. If persons in difficulty happen to belong to an active religious congregation, they may be fortunate enough to have a priest, minister, or rabbi who knows how to listen. Although no one today would confuse a priest with the psychiatrist, there was a time when they were one and the same. Clerics can still be a big help.

People today recognize the psychiatrist as a physician who specializes in "nervous" disorders, i.e., all those many manifestations of what used to be included globally under the phrase "bad nerves." Psychiatry is a branch of medicine and, like other members of the medical brotherhood, the psychiatrist uses a philosophical structure known as the medical model to understand disturbances in life. Physical causes are assumed to be at the root of symptoms, and physical agents in the form of medications are provided for relief. There is plenty of talk in psychiatry about mental disease, but the understanding of "mental" tends to be very physical: i.e., brain, nerves, neurochemistry, electricity. The critics of medicalized psychiatry claim that its exclusive concern with physical causes and effects is an inadequate way of understanding the human condition.

The priest (minister or rabbi), we all know, is different. Like the psychiatrist, he works with people but employs different categories to diagnose their difficulties and uses a different therapy to bring about a cure. Rather than resorting to physical agents like shock or chemical agents like thorazine, he makes use of talk as a therapy and spends time looking at reasons and motives in order to understand difficulties. Instead of using terms like "patient" and "mental disease," he speaks of penitents and people in distress. Priests don't talk of persons being possessed by spirits any more, but they may very well ask, "What has gotten into you?"

There was an age, before our own, when there were no psychiatrists as we know them. In medieval times the function performed by the psychiatrist was taken care of by the priest. All the "shrinking" that went on took place in the same small soundproof "offices" called confessionals. It was the business of the priest to minister to people who were pained by conflict or guilt or grief, or whose behavior had gone astray, or whose life was out of control. The priestly minister, not unlike today's secular helpers, needed stature and authority in order to carry out his mission, and this came from the "power to loose and to bind." There was a nice simple division of labor back then between the priest and physician which had real social advantages and which rested upon a widely accepted assumption of the separation of body and soul, the spiritual and the physical, rationality and corporeal embodiment.

Those days may seem long gone, and yet in a sense they are still with us. It is still difficult to know whether we should go to the physician in order to treat a depression with medication, or to a therapist of the word who uses talk to help us discover the sources of the anger or guilt which we are turning against ourselves. In medieval times the confessor would handle the guilt and anger while the physician would perhaps provide some timely assistance in the form of a dose of chloral for relaxation. We don't know where to go because today we are still unclear about the lines between the spiritual and the physical, and we are especially unclear about their interaction upon one another.

In medieval times there was no problem of choosing between the priest and the physician. They may have been separate, but they were not in competition, and consequently there was no sense of having to choose between rivals. In the confessional penitents were presumed to be able to do something about their behavior because they were agents and therefore responsible to a degree. In the office of the physician their troubles were assumed to have happened to them, making them "patients" rather than agents.

Things may have been simpler then, but in our more sophisticated age the basic questions and uncertainties have not gone away. Lurking behind our more complex division of labor and the proliferation of healers are the age-old questions of active and passive, responsibility for conduct; accounts of behavior based on reasons and motives versus the scientific accounts based on causes and mechanisms. Our society is more complex than the medieval one when it comes to social roles, but we have not made much progress on the underlying philosophical questions about human conduct. We remain as much in doubt as ever about human autonomy.

There is no way to settle these enduring questions, but we can make the assumption that the person who is not seriously ill still has some control over his behavior. We can assume that persons are agents, that even feelings are open to modifications, and that talk is beneficial to those who are caught in upsetting situations. If feelings are to be modified and the areas of life over which a person still exercises some agency are to be expanded, then more attention has to be paid to the importance of talk. A personal experience will illustrate this point.

I ran into a man not long ago who was on the brink of a breakdown. We met casually at a movie. Years before we had both been involved in a reading group, and although we were not close friends, we knew one another. It was he who opened the conversation with an inquiry about my health. He heard I had been sick and expressed his surprise and sympathy.

After explaining that I was beginning to feel better, I asked how he had been. He looked considerably older, and his face showed the marks of some recent physical violence. My inquiry precipitated an immediate change in his whole presence. His head dropped, his voice became unstable, his eyes quickly filled with tears, and he began to tell about an impending divorce. In the midst of this terrible ordeal, he had been assaulted and badly beaten, and this experience not only left ugly physical marks on his body, but, even worse, had just about destroyed his already weakened self-esteem. Then, to top it off, he was at a crucial period of professional training when the heaviest demands were being made on him for competent performance.

If stress levels could be measured objectively, this poor fellow's tension would register at the outer edge of the danger area. He was literally about to crack up.

After listening to as much of the story as the place and time would permit, I asked if there was anyone he could talk to during this ordeal. "No," he said, "What good would that do? Talking to someone is not going to help a bit with all my problems."

I am convinced that if I had been a physician and offered him a pill, he would have accepted it gratefully and taken it with confidence. More than he knew, this person was typical of many in our culture. Even his problems were typical, though he suffered them in an extreme degree. And the attitude that chemistry really helps, but talk does not, is so common that it qualifies as assumed wisdom (especially among contemporary males). It is possible that in a culture that considers itself advanced and sophisticated, people have forgotten some of the basic truths about human nature?

The ancients knew about the power of the word and the therapeutic benefits of conversation. But we seem to have forgotten this. Before there were so many pills and potions, what curing took place was done by talk. In the very ancient cultures there were specialized therapeutic words in the forms of charms, and prayers, spells, and cheering speech. Later in more literary periods the ancients developed more technical types of therapeutic speech and conversation. Both Plato and Aristotle, for example, dedicated many pages to the topic of therapy by word, offering systematic explanations of just how understanding, which develops through talking things out, actually effects a cure.

The poor fellow I ran into was not only in very serious condition, but because of a cultural impoverishment he did not know about the most basic and primitive forms of help that were available to him as a human being. Man is a talking animal, and talk, among its many other characteristics, is therapeutic. If the listening person is a trained professional, so much the better, but therapy can take place even if he isn't. Just a sympathetic and intelligent listener can be a great help. There is such a thing as self-help, and a lot of real help comes from friends, family, teachers, and clerics.

Many who read this will sympathize with the man I met at the movie. They agree with him and share his attitude. When they think about getting help for a problem, they think both about something physical and something total. When he said to me, "What good will it do to talk?" he meant that talking would not solve everything. And who could disagree?

But most real problems do not have complete solutions. We have to live with many unsatisfactory and unresolvable situations. It is, however, a shame that we ignore or have forgotten what human beings in other times knew very well: a little help is a lot of help; talk is therapeutic; feelings which are talked about can be better controlled and better understood; and if the person with whom you talk happens to be an intelligent listener, you stand a good chance of ending up the talk session with much greater control over your life.

Talking about feelings makes a difference because talk provides the context for thinking about the feelings, what causes them, and how we handle them. A colleague of mine stands as a monument to the benefits of thinking through our feeling states.

Phil Buono, in the estimation of everyone who knows him, is a very attractive man. Physically he looks awful. His six-foot frame carries only about 150 pounds; his face has deep lines; where once there was hair, now there are just some very thin strings. But after you know him, he becomes downright attractive. His internal goodness and attractive ways come through the gawky appearance and beautify it.

Phil was brought up in Pittsburgh. His dad worked in the steel mills. Without any financial help from home he managed to get a Ph.D. and heads up an undergraduate department of social work. He spends a lot of time with his students, helping them with their clinical work and community assignments. His classes are interesting, and he is respected by his colleagues for being warm and fair and very competent. He has many close friends and a good family life.

Phil had what we would describe as a deprived childhood, both economically and psychologically. His dad was aloof and generally unavailable. Periodically he would go on alcoholic binges, and the sight of his drunken father terrorized the young boy. His mother was a very nervous woman who worried a lot and was often very irritable. Although she was consistently available to her son, she was not able to provide him with much security, and Phil grew up shy and insecure.

As he developed, however, he made the best of his situation rather than sulking or using his parents as excuses for not performing. He worked hard in school, made good grades, and gradually made his way through graduate school. Now Phil is able to talk about his parents in a realistic way, but he harbors no anger or resentment against them. Somehow he developed strength enough even to acknowledge and accept his parents' shortcomings.

Rather than nursing hurts or concentrating on his problems, Phil developed an authentic concern for other people's problems. Other members of the department still act like adolescents in their self-centeredness and preoccupation with their own affairs. He, on the other hand, is the father figure, standing above the rest in authority while serving them in their needs.

How can Phil be explained? How did he manage to overcome both hereditary and environmental factors to become such a mature and attractive person? How did he avoid becoming aloof and alcoholic like his dad? Why did he pattern his life around helping others rather than self-protection? How did he manage to convert the nervousness he got from his mother into productivity instead of irritation?

Was it the influence of teachers along the way after whom he tried to model himself? Was it the result of personalities he came across in the books he read as a child with his mother and continued to read and discuss with her all throughout his adolescent years? Was it some very important choice he made at some point to become a certain type person and then remade over and over again after every failure? Was it the help he received from a prayer life which began as a small child? Who knows?

More than likely all of the above played a part in this life that turned out so well. The good influences, the crucial choices, the prayer life were surely the most important influences. But Phil never gave up on reading, and some of his reading about the human condition certainly had an impact on him. He was both a feeling person and a person who thought about feelings. To some extent at least Phil avoided the worst reactions and chose the healthiest ones because he had "a leg up" on his feelings. Rather than having feelings dictate his behavior, he understood his feelings and was able to get the best out of them. It is with the hope that a little thinking about this aspect of humanness will do us all well that we turn to a few thoughts on different feeling states.

2. Feeling Conflicted

People who have conflicts frequently think they are the only ones in tough straits. Everyone they see along the street appears to be well-adjusted. The successful and the well-to-do especially give the appearance of having everything together. The truth, however, is that everyone has troubles, and the most successful are oftentimes the most conflicted.

A very prominent lawyer, with a national reputation for tough courtroom fighting, is tyrannized by a bitter, hostile, and angry wife whom he cannot manage and cannot get away from.

A newspaper publisher has a powerful position, a very lush salary, and a nice wife and children. He looks like the paradigm of success, and yet he is incapable of resisting any and every opportunity to tumble into bed with a younger woman. He gets quite a few opportunities and has to be dragged out feet first from one mess after the other in order to avoid ruin.

A professor is a world authority on nuclear chemistry, but all he wants to talk about is his health. One would think that he has everything together, but in fact he is deathly afraid of falling apart. He worries about his diet, the weather, exercise; and every little body ache is the basis for panic about some awful incurable illness. The fact is that most people are less than together and even the high and the mighty are troubled by painful conflict. Impulsive sex and compulsive worry are only two examples of high-priced, low-yield coping devices for these painful pushes and pulls. Excess alcohol and drug use are probably the most common examples of the costly ways of handling confict.

The behaviors of some conflicted people are costly because they are self-defeating. Time and again, conflicted persons do themselves in. Traps are laid, not by others, but by themselves. Although they are twenty, thirty, forty, or fifty years old, they continue to react to persons and problems the same way they did at age two, three, four, or five. Everybody can tell something is wrong. Some can even see that there is a correlation between present problems and childhood happenings.

If only the conflicted person could see that the behaviors which keep his life in turmoil are substitutions for something else, then the stage would be set for making some changes in his life. It is the lack of any insight about feelings and the troublesome behaviors they generate that keeps a conflicted person imprisoned in his own jail.

In some cases conflict comes from being torn among a variety of personal wants. Great battles go on inside between opposing possibilities. "I want sex that is satisfying, but I do not want close intimate relationships." "I want a close intimate relationship, but I do not want sex." "I want security and permanence, but I do not want to settle down to one job." "I like Harry and consider him a possible partner, but I'm afraid someone else will come along whom I'll like more." "I hate my job, but I am afraid to change." "I want to eat, but hate my fat looks."

A happier, less conflicted person makes his choices and

lives with them. If he decides to eat his cake, he doesn't expect to have it. But the conflicted person can't decide. He wants one thing and its opposite. He creates his own pain, lays his own traps, constructs his own obstacles, and generally makes his life miserable, no matter how much people try to help him. Headaches, stomach aches, nervousness, allergies, frigidity, and even more serious ailments may be caused by inner conflicts. He or she may complain a lot, but reject every effort to help.

There is no way of avoiding conflicts in this life, but there are better and worse ways of working them through. Unnecessary conflict, on the other hand, creates unnecessary struggle which uses up precious energy and pollutes the pleasant pools of personal satisfaction which provide a relief from life's drudgery. Trying to understand our conflicts and our struggles can pay off in some nice dividends.

Many of us carry around in our adult heads childhood expectations that life should be a never-ending succession of delights, and this makes conflict inevitable and adjustment very difficult. Fairy tales can continue into adulthood as unrealistic expectations. If this happens and the outside environment forces us to struggle because it is unfriendly, harsh, critical, or demanding, we can wind up feeling unfairly treated. Adding to the sense of betrayal is the conflict we often have about the kind of person we should be: whether to be selfish or unselfish, honest or dishonest, to be grown up or immature, to be parents or to live just for ourselves.

Everyone who has lived any time at all knows that life is a struggle, but some continue to respond to this fact as if it were an unjust imposition. The fact of stuggle embitters some people, and ineffectual responses to it turn them into unhappy neurotics. No psychiatrist can explain why one person uses conflict and struggle to make herself into a saint and

make a sonnet out of life, while another person in similar circumstances becomes neurotic or some other variety of
chronic complainer.

The neurotic not only thinks that he should not have conflicts or have to struggle like the rest of humankind, but to
hear him talk, you would think that he was in life all alone.
Others either do not count or count very little. Everything
centers on his conflicted feelings and his struggles with an unfriendly world. There is little or no awareness of what other
people are going through and little concern about the effect
of his behavior on them. Constant conflict and unnecessary
struggle over every problem put an unbearable strain on personal relations.

Because relationships are so thin and superficial, the neurotic learns very little from other people. Fooling oneself is
preferred to realistic self-assessment. Conflicts are not recognized, struggles are not analyzed, and responsibility for failure is not accepted. The sicker the person, the more his real
situation is denied, and the less chance there is that others can
break through to him. Inability to handle the conflicts and
struggle of life is closely linked with inability to be objective
about one's own life or to maintain warm friendships.

Certain behaviors signal the neurotic response to life. They
provide reliable evidence that there is something wrong. The
seriousness of the problem depends upon the intensity and
persistence of these signal behaviors which are responses we
all make on occasion. If our life is dominated by conflicts and
struggle, however, we will recognize ourselves in all the
behaviors.

1. Always worrying
2. Unable to concentrate for no obvious reason

3. Unhappy in the absence of real tragedy
4. Becoming angry easily and often
5. Unable to get to sleep or waking up at 3:00 or 4:00 A.M.
6. Wide mood swings from depression to unexplained elation
7. Prefer not to be with other people
8. Unable to be around children
9. Unable to handle changes or upsets in a schedule
10. Constantly bitter and resentful of others
11. Afraid in unthreatening situations
12. Always right and others always wrong
13. Suffering from aches and pains which doctors cannot diagnose

One danger in making such a list is that suggestible persons will see themselves everywhere and make themselves sick worrying that now, on top of everything else, they are neurotic. This possible bad effect is offset, I hope, by the advantages that some will gain from an opportunity to take a more objective look at their lives. Just knowing about these danger signals will be enough to move some people away from them. Recognizing the signs of bad adjustment can be enough to gain insight into the conflict and struggle which cause the behavior.

Struggle and conflict there are in every life. We all need to be reminded of this from time to time because unconsciously we not only want to live forever, but we want to be eternally happy. These benefits may await us as the fruit of salvation, but they certainly cannot be expected here and now. And yet even here God wants us to enjoy his gift of creation. Constant struggle and conflict may be unsaintly forms of ingratitude.

3. Feeling Depressed

There is more than one way of coming to be depressed. It would be nice if every case of depression were the result of the same underlying cause. If there were only one motive, drive, conflict, or loss which always lead to the symptoms of depression, then the treatment would be directed at that underlying cause and have a good chance of success. This, however, is not the case.

One of the major difficulties with psychiatric diagnosis is ignorance of specific underlying causes. Life, we know, is not simple. And depression, like everything else in life, is complex beyond the capability of any one theory to understand it. As a result, to understand depression, we have to understand the whole life situation of each depressed person—no small task indeed. A theory about depression, by comparison, is simple.

Nevertheless, some cases of depression do fall into clusters, and certain theoretical formulae do help make sense of them. We can never understand a unique person by applying a general theory, but a theory can help us get started with the task of figuring out why I (John, Mary, Bill, or Margaret) get depressed.

Many depressions are related to the themes of development, i.e., a particular stage in life when a person is expected to take the next step forward toward independence and autonomy. There may be joy and excitement about such a step on the one hand, but at the same time there is often fear and insecurity. And for some people the latter feelings dominate. They feel inept and uncertain. The next stage of life may involve a series of new demands, all of which taken together seem overwhelming. And depression is a very common response to such change.

Besides, every step forward means a loss. The child of school age loses the former intimacy with his mother, as well as the comforts and supports of home. And the six-year-old, excited about all that awaits him at the big school building but clinging to his mother's hand and not wanting to lose her company, symbolizes each of us at every new stage of life. Even the young child, when threatened by the next state of development, may get depressed.

Events in the very early life of a child can set up a fertile ground for depression so that there is an internal readiness for a depressive response when things go wrong later on. This disposition to depression is not the person's fault; in fact, it may be no one's fault. It could have been created by the death of a parent, or by an unavoidable parental absence at a particularly difficult time in the child's life.

At very early stages of life a child may feel the loss of a significant person very deeply but be unable to mourn or to resolve ambivalence toward the absent person. It could even happen that the child was unable to differentiate himself from the missing person, thereby experiencing his very self as lost. For the young child, the parent is inevitably overidealized and overevaluated. Consequently, a real or imagined loss of the parent constitutes a terrible trauma. If sufficiently intense it may lead to a fragile personality structure which is vulnerable, all through life, to loss. Disappointment later on, or sadness, or even guilt can trigger off that early injury and lead to depression.

Because every child inevitably suffers losses in the process of growing up, everybody is somewhat vulnerable to depression. We all had to grow through the loss of paradise, when child and mother are one and every need is gratified. Growing up to where the child realizes that he is separate from the mother is experienced as a loss of the mother and causes a corresponding set of depressive feelings.

The process of development continues, and at every stage there are new losses and responses to them which we may describe as temporary or transitional depressions. Separation from home and mother at school age is one such developmental stage which symbolizes both the ambivalence and the conflict associated with every next step.

Adolescence is another tough period. There is a new round of separations and demands for individuation and maturation which very often are accompanied by depressive reactions. There are instances in which the adolescent becomes clinically and pathologically depressed, requiring professional intervention, but these are sometimes difficult to distinguish from what might be described as the normal, temporary depressions which accompany development at this stage. Teenages are hard to live with because they are frequently hostile, aggressive, and withdrawn, i.e., they are depressed. They are working through the losses of an earlier stage and trying to manage fears of what lies ahead.

And the normal, transient depressions do not stop after adolescence. Others may occur when leaving home for college. Marriage, a happy affair, may entail depression. Even having a child involves a transient loss in the sense of a physical separation from the child within and sometimes a transient depression. And then there are the losses of middle age and old age. And on and on. . . .

And it is not just development with its losses and distasteful aspects but often good and exciting things that cause depression. It is not at all unusual that a promotion or a marriage or a new job we had been hoping for precipitates the enigmatic depressed feelings.

Every really significant event, including the happy ones, represents a development which has a frightening side: the new demands, the inevitable loss, the separation, the uncertainties, the possibilities for failure. Even those persons whom everyone judges to be strong and superior and secure have underlying fears about their "real" strength, their "real" worth, their "real" competence. Failure in reaching idealized aspirations for ourselves can cause depression, but in some cases the very chance of failure inherent in a promotion, or a long-awaited achievement, is enough to trigger off these painful down feelings.

In many instances, then, a depression can be traced to an underlying sense of weakness in the face of requirements to move ahead. Most of us are not heroes. Advancing even in the sense of growing up causes fear. And in response we tend to step back, withdraw, and get bogged down. Just understanding how this happens can be enough to start a move out of the doldrums.

In one theoretical formula despression amounts to a feeling of helplessness and dependency for which we are ashamed. The longer we stay withdrawn or give in to the fears, the less we think of ourselves, the less capable we feel to take the next step, the more confused we become about what to do next, and the more depressed we feel. In the worst cases of depression, people literally give up on development and any form of movement to the next step in life. For these, professional help should be sought.

Feelings predominate in depression, but not to the exclusion of thought and thought patterns. In fact, we could say that besides being a mood disorder depression is also a thought disorder. But thinking that goes astray can be returned to healthier ways.

The depressed person does not suffer hallucinations or loss of cognitive contact with time and place, but he tends to engage in what is referred to as dichotomous thinking, i.e., things are either black or white, all or nothing at all. A businessman, for example, may suffer a single reversal and begin to think of himself as a total failure. Or a writer may do a book which is not a best-seller and consider himself a complete flop. The negative experience is exaggerated, and then overgeneralizations are drawn. There is such a concentration on the negative that many positive elements are either overlooked or discounted. This type thought disturbance is not the bizarre thinking of schizophrenia. It tends to be more discrete. However, once cognitive distortions are in place, the down mood and bad thinking begin to reinforce one another.

Another aspect of disturbed cognition in depressed patients involves thought about the future. It is characteristic of depression that the future is thought of as hopeless or full of only negative experience. A young woman, twenty-five years old and not unattractive, thinks her life is not worth living. She cannot come up with solutions to her problems. Suicide emerges as the only way out of her difficulties. And she is not untypical.

The totally negative interpretation of experience and the completely negative view of the future are cornerstones of depressions. Other aspects of depression such as low self-esteem, self-criticism, feelings of deprivation, and suicidal thoughts are all related to the distorted thoughts about present and future experience. Depression actually stands for a complete way of being in the world.

Many different forms of distorted and illogical thinking are used by depressed people. I'll mention just a few:

Arbitrary inference: i.e., the patient draws negative inferences or negative interpretations from statements made to him that were in no way negative.

Selective abstraction: i.e., focusing on negative details of conversation and experience, even though they are extraneous.

Overgeneralization: i.e., global negative conclusions about oneself based on one incident.

Magnification and minimization: i.e., errors in interpretation that exaggerate experience out of all rational proportion.

If distorted interpretation is part of the disease, then improved interpretation has to be part of the cure. One of the greatest benefits of having a good talk with a friend or a priest comes in the form of help with our thinking process.

Getting one's head screwed on a little straighter is always a great leap forward. Thinking helps.

4. Feeling Anxious

Before Freud's influence populated our language with fancy terms, people who were not well emotionally were referred to as being nervous. Some people were naturally more nervous than others. Sometimes a string of bad luck would make a person nervous. A woman might become nervous after the loss of her husband. Work sometimes got on a man's nerves.

Today we use different terms. We speak more about anxiety than about nerves. What has not changed, however, is the fact that human beings are often threatened, easily intimidated, and always in danger of falling apart under pressure.

It is not just the three-year-old who is terrified by a world full of threats. To some extent we never get beyond three years old. Everyone can draw up a long list of awful things that could very well happen to him. Our dreams are full of such occurrences. And in addition to the real, rational, justifiable threats that are part of every life, there are the many times we feel anxious for no known reason.

Actually the anxiety we feel without having an explanation of its source is the most painful and threatening of all to bear. Rationalization is a device people use to identify a cause. Even if it is not the real reason, finding a source legitimates the anxiety and in some sense relieves its pain.

Displacement is another common technique for managing the vague anxiety whose source we ignore. Not to know the cause leaves a person doubly vulnerable. So, to displace the underlying and unknown threat onto a snake, or wolf, or whatever, provides a degree of relief. All one has to do is to avoid the phobic object.

Somatization is another management technique in which the anxiety is related to a physical condition (e.g., digestion or a backache) and responsibility for handling it is transferred to a physician.

Not everyone, however, makes use of Freudian defenses like rationalization, displacement, and somatization. We are all threatened by feelings of vulnerability, weakness, impotence. Everyone has the hidden fear that he will be found out and his weakness exposed. One standard response is simply to try to increase strength and power. People try to become more efficient, or learned, or competent. Reassurance is sought from friends. Positions of power are pursued. One gets involved in activities which demonstrates superiority. All these are techniques to relieve anxiety.

But life is not just a series of serious productive efforts. A less productive and more gratifying technique for managing vague distress is spending money. A little extravagance, whether on oneself or someone else, is a display of power, a proof of worth, and a very common way of alleviating anxiety.

Eating is another common mechanism of management. If anxiety is a vague pain, then eating is an easily available painkiller. The child at mother's breast is a classic symbol of relieved anxiety. Since presumably we have all had that sense of childhood peace and contentment, it is no wonder many try to regain it. Putting something in the mouth is a prevalent way of relieving anxiety. Cigarettes are often substitutes for childhood cookies. And when an attempt is made to give up cigarettes—look out, cookie jar!

And finally, sex can be a way of gaining relief from anxiety. Ideally an expression of love, sexual acts are easily directed to other functions. Adolescent masturbation, for example, is more frequently a way of allaying anxiety than a means of attaining gratification.

It is one thing to understand many of the ways people use to relieve anxiety; it is another thing to try to identify the source of human anxiety. The nineteenth century philosopher Nietzsche had insisted that because survival is always a struggle anything that calls into question our power or confidence fills us with dread and anxiety.

Freud translated Nietzsche's idea into his term, castration anxiety. Because of Freud's influence on our culture, this phrase has become a part of everyday vocabulary. Taken literally, it seems ridiculous. Who today has any experience of someone approaching his genitals with a carving knife? But metaphorically, castration anxiety refers to all the many threats to a person's power and ability to cope. Male genitals can symbolize power even in a culture less dominated by males and more subtle about its aggression.

Males and females can feel threats to power and its corresponding anxiety when money is lost, because money is power in our society. Even the threat of losing money is enough to cause a gnawing and physically destructive anxiety.

Or if a person feels he is not performing well at work he can feel anxious and threatened, because work performance and its rewards are power. Think of the power attached to certain positions and what the president or superintendent would be like, stripped of his role. Few persons are secure enough in themselves to give up the power associated with social and economic positions. Great anxiety is generated even by the thought of someone, who is after "my job."

Even something like a receding hairline can cause anxiety, because aging is linked with a loss of power in our youth-centered culture. Correspondingly, the woman who notices a wrinkle is intimidated and anxiety-ridden because her power is associated with beauty. All those "magical" creams which "make skin look young" appeal to deep-seated threats to power which is the focus of feelings of dread and anxiety.

Criticism is so dreaded because it is a frontal attack on our power. But the threat to power that causes such dread and anxiety need not be so direct. Hearing about someone forty years old who died of a heart attack is an indirect threat, but enough to cause anxiety. It reminds us of our weakness and personal vulnerability. Sometimes the threat to our power is so indirect as not to be consciously noted, and we don't know what is causing the discomfort. "I don't know why I feel so anxious today" is something we have heard and likely have said.

Someone passing us on the street without speaking can cause anxiety. An invitation we did not receive can do the same. Approval and acceptance are forms of power, and threats to them cause anxiety. We may be adults, but we never completely get over the linkage between power and lovableness which is so clear to the small child. As long as he is loved by the parent he is powerful and safe, but withdrawal of love means a loss of this power. And being unloved or unapproved or unaccepted continues to threaten us as adults. The most imagined sense of unlovableness, the most incidental suggestion of unacceptability, the most accidental oversight or disapproval is all that is needed to constitute an assault to our power and generate anxiety.

After looking at coping devices and sources of anxiety can we now provide a definition of anxiety? Trying to define anxiety is like trying to define space and time. We know what it is until someone asks us to define it. If pressed to explain an emotion, we usually resort to the "you know how you feel when . . ." technique. It is incredibly difficult to conceptualize and then communicate with clarity even the most commonly experienced emotions. And yet it is worth a try, because coming to understand our emotions is a giant step toward gaining some control over them.

Perhaps we can start by stating the obvious: anxiety is related to fear. It may be understood as an aspect of fear which occurs in a special way in special situations. Fear ranges from trepidation to terror, perturbation to panic, and anxiety belongs to the lower ranges. In higher or more intense forms we use words other than anxiety to describe the fearing condition, e.g., alarm.

It is also worth mentioning that the fear responses as well as the other human emotions are built into the human animal and have very important survival functions. Reflecting an awesome intelligence, the body responds automatically in the face of danger so that both survival and security are enhanced. Around danger, the most adaptive behaviors are indicated by our feelings, which direct us toward the best course of action.

All higher animals have fear response, but generally they seem narrowly tied to specific dangers. Not so in man. His intelligence makes the world in which the human being lives enormous. It embraces the tiniest atom, the immense universe, and every other form of life. Man's mind enlarges his environment and expands his awareness of danger. No wonder he is so afraid.

But what about the adaptive behavior set off by fear? Multiple physiological changes occur automatically to prepare the body either for fight or flight in the face of what is dangerous. The automatic nervous system pumps adrenalin into the blood, heart and blood pressure increase, palms sweat, pupils dilate, blood flow is redirected. All these changes facilitate survival. Or do they?

The causes of fear in man are both conscious and unconscious. Besides the specific dangerous things we are aware of, there are the unspecific, generalized, oftentimes unknown dangers. These produce the low range of fear we call anxiety and a low-grade version of the physiological changes we listed.

Anxiety then may be defined as a vague and indirect fear which has no specific source. We may be anxious and tense and not know why. (Then we remember we have a trip coming up on Korean Air, and our anxiety turns into fear.)

A vague, unspecific, and possibly even unconscious, anxiety in some people is continuous. Then the changes it triggers, rather than being helpful for survival, cause wear and tear on both the body and mind of man. Adaptive reactions evoked in occasional dangerous situations, if maintained over a long period, cause serious physiological and mental illness. Understanding anxiety is one way of modifying its potential for harm in our life.

5. Feeling Spiteful

When we were kids there was one response for every hurt inflicted by another: "I'll get you back."

Getting back is sometimes referred to as "talionic" morality, a word which comes from scripture. The *"lex talionis,"* or talionic law, stipulates a tit-for-tat response to injury.

As a matter of fact, the eye-for-eye, tooth-for-tooth way of behaving was an ethical advance over more primitive forms of behavior which condoned massive retaliation. In psychiatric jargon, however, it has come to stand for the moral stance of a very young person, before he or she learns to forgive and forget.

But not everyone manages to move beyond this early stage of moral development. In some cases, "getting back," or spite, becomes embedded in the personality so deeply that it dominates even adult experience. More adult and mature expressions of morality are simply not achieved, and correspondingly all the benefits of ethical development are missed.

Instead of life being characterized by positive feelings which are associated with healthy happiness, it is polluted with negative feelings which both cause and constitute illness and unhappiness.

For a kid, getting back is not a life strategy, but rather a specific response directed against someone or something for a specific injury. Once the score is evened up and the offender punished, that is the end of the desire for revenge in a child. Getting back for kids oftentimes has a very playful tone.

But not so the feelings of spite in older people. There is nothing playful or healthy about the person whose impulse to get back becomes a permanent feeling state. Rather than being connected to specific reasons and distinct events, it can become a standard response elicited as much by a kindly act as by hurtful or critical ones. Such is the distortion of this style of life, in fact, that good turns are even more sure to elicit a spiteful response. Even the smile of a spiteful man becomes a way of putting someone down. Every gesture flowing from such a permanently negative feeling state is contaminated.

The cynic, for example, gets back at everyone, but he saves his deepest cuts and sharpest blows for those whom others admire. It is the good man whom he most abhors. The inevitable negative side of every good character and the faults of every good man constitute a sort of special prey for him, one for which the cynic has developed a special sense and a special skill in destroying. No longer is a specific injury or cause required for engaging the impulse to get back. Now it operates automatically and as a fixed pattern.

One of the most popular disguises of spite are high-sounding moral expressions. A great deal of "getting back" takes the form of "virtuous outrage" at some injury or threat. Pious words and high-sounding rhetoric become a vehicle for indulging the old impulse to get back at the hated other. Sometimes the pious and self-righteous distinguish themselves by an uncanny capacity to keep alive seething hostility for years. Religious idealism and ethical demeanor can be one grand facade for unholy feelings and motivations.

The next time you waste an evening watching the popular television programs, notice how often getting back or getting even makes up the underlying theme of the show. First there is some wrong done, and then a string of events follow which finally even things up. We may give lip service on Sunday to the notion that vengeance is reserved to God, but as a matter of fact we spend a great deal of our lives making sure God doesn't slip up and let some wrong go unaddressed.

The question we have to ask ourselves, however, is whether taking over God's job is good for our mental health. Is getting back a healthy way to live? Or is it in fact a way of inflicting death on ourselves as we inflict justice on others?

One thing is sure: the impulse to get back is one we all recognize. It is known to every child, as well as to every adult. Statistically, it can be called normal, and yet there is evidence beyond doubting that in certain intensities it becomes an illness, serious enough to cause death. Not only are people killed to get even, but suicide, too, occurs for the same reason.

It would be more accurate to say that human beings, like most animals, have a natural capacity for aggression. There are times when one's territory or home or loved ones must be protected against attack. And only naive persons try to organize their lives on the assumption that there is no evil and therefore no reason ever to show aggression.

What makes spite different is what it adds to aggression. Aggression subsides once the danger is removed. Getting back and getting even continue the aggression long after the situation which stimulated it has subsided. A capacity for aggression is natural to man, but there is nothing natural about continued vindictiveness.

And nature provides no real satisfactions or supports for spiteful or continuingly aggressive people. They may experience some satisfaction in making fun of others or when their spiteful strategies are successful. But these satisfactions never add up to anything like happiness.

But recognition is not the whole answer. Sometimes an in-

grained habit has to be changed. Then quiet thought about
the example of a Jewish prophet from the beginning of our
era may be helpful. He was not spiteful and did not get back,
and gave his followers a command to imitate the attitude he
demonstrated even toward those who hated him.

What may start out as an individual decision to take revenge can gradually turn into a spiteful spirit. One moves
from a commitment to get back at this or that one to a generalized negative way of being that colors every experience. The
negative feelings little by little apply even to persons who
have done no hurt or injury. The impulse to revenge becomes
more deep-seated until it becomes a part of the character of
the person. As such it is ready to express itself in any and all
circumstances.

Spite as a life strategy creates a detracting character which
is morally deficient in that it lacks love and is incapable of
forgiveness. In fact, for the spiteful person just a plain old-
fashioned emotional expression becomes impossible. If such
a person could just come out and call someone an SOB right
to his face, or shake a fist, or throw a punch, such acts would
relieve much of the inner pollution and begin a healing process. But restraint is the cornerstone of this character structure just as surely as this character structure is grounded in
impotence. The underlying weakness is both ethical and psychological.

As time goes by the whole personality of the spiteful person
is poisoned and embittered. Never able to muster the strength
to strike out in order to even things up, the spiteful person
becomes a hidden detractor, joined by some ironic bond to
all those more successful persons against whom he plans and
schemes. Little by little the negative feelings draw out the
oxygen of the soul, leaving behind a dried-up, embittered,
and thoroughly spiritless person. The silent hater, the detrac-

tor, the spiteful character becomes as ugly to himself as he or she is to others.

Some sins carry their own punishment and some sins, when left to fester, create downright sick people.

Harry was a twenty-three-year-old college dropout. As a child he had been abused by a hostile mother and a passive father. Now he was unable to study and would not work. Just beneath the surface were pools of anger and aggression that kept him from doing anything constructive with his life. He was furious with his parents and, being unable to hurt them directly, turned his hostility toward himself in alcohol and drug abuse and all sorts of disruptive and destructive behavior.

Soon after beginning a job or school, he would do something to destroy the possible gain. His character was permeated by spite, and for him the only way to get back at his parents was to become so pathetic that they would have to take care of him.

Harry couldn't get better because he had to "get back." Spite, which we recognize as an ethical category, had become the core of psychiatric pathology.

Scripture and theological commentary have had as much to say about spite as psychiatric sources. Putting the understanding of both traditions together can provide us with good insight into this form of coping and help us avoid its most harmful effects. Both traditions understand spite to be a reactive impulse. It is preceded by an attack or injury, either real or imagined.

Anger and indignation accompany spite, but spite is not the same as an act of self-defense or an immediate reprisal. The immediate response is checked, and a "just wait" strategy becomes the essential ingredient of revenge. Blockage and postponement is adopted as a strategy because of fear of defeat. Spite, then, is intimately linked to impotence. It is a strategy of weakness.

Weakness also dictates the accompanying strategy of tit-for-tat. Largess and forgiveness are alien to the person whose personality is characterized by revenge.

Spite tends to be experienced time and again because the anger suppressed in it is always there, along with the fear of taking action. As such, it becomes deeply embedded in a person's character. So situated, spite becomes a central motive and characteristic of the person's experience. Spite nourishes many negative emotions, hateful impulses, and hostile acts. If it is intense enough and pervasive enough, spite creates serious pathology. In weaker forms, it makes unhappy lives and sour experience.

If getting back is not natural and is proven to be the cause of much physical and mental distress, how do we control it in our lives? How can we keep it within bounds? How can we avoid the physical and psychic pain it causes? How can we recognize the situation in which getting back is too costly and therefore must be left to God for our own sanity?

This may be the task of a lifetime rather than a single project. It is helpful, however, to be able to recognize spite for what it is and to realize that it is harmful to our health.

6. Feeling Shame or Guilt

Jean Paul Sartre, the well-known French existential philosopher, in one of his books describes a scene in which a male character was stooped over, peeking through a keyhole of a hotel room. Suddenly, interest and enjoyment changed to discomfort and then, little by little, into pain. Without changing position or looking around, he could feel someone's eyes on him. The other person, by his look, destroyed the pleasure of voyeurism. The look of the other changed the voyeur from someone looking to someone looked at, and with this change came a cluster of uncomfortable feelings which we use the word shame to describe.

Sartre's peeping Tom might have felt guilt later on that evening, even if no one had discovered him, but it took the look of another to create the experience of shame. Guilt is something of a private feeling which begins and ends within the subject. But shame requires others. Both guilt and shame are associated with moral failures, sins, or misdeeds. Shame, however, is much more a social phenomenon. To feel shame one has to be involved in a community and be capable of relationship.

Some anthropologists distinguish between cultures which control social misconduct through guilt and others which rely upon shame and public dishonor. In shame cultures only those bad deeds which are seen by others are bothersome. Dishonor and disgrace are the foundations of morality. Guilt cultures represent a cultural advance in the sense that in them individuals control their behavior independently of the looks of others. But individuals rarely become so isolated as to lose all sense of shame. And if they do, psychiatric standards begin to function, and the shameless person is considered deficient to the point of being mentally ill.

Even very social animals like dogs show signs of something like shame. My dog, Erasmus, lowers both head and tail and slinks down when caught in some misbehavior. He may look like he is ashamed, but I think he actually is only feeling fear. Once I give him the slightest hint that there will be no bad consequences visited on him, his vital, happy signs return and that's the end of shame-like behavior. Erasmus, I think, is just afraid of punishment.

We human animals, however, feel the pain of shame even when we know that there will be no punishment visited upon us. We are pained by the shame itself. Sometimes we would feel better if there were some punishment administered which would amend for our disgrace.

The stronger the sense of community, the more prominent will be the role of shame. People who live anonymous lives in large urban centers rarely experience the shame which people feel who belong to a community and feel responsibility to the group. The Puritans, for example, had a very tight-knit community structure, and shame played a major role in their lives. Good meant good in the eyes of the community, and evil was synonymous with dishonor or the loss of community esteem.

Hawthorne's Hester Prynne, wearing that scarlet letter, would mean nothing to modern New Yorkers. But Hester lived in a community where people knew one another, and she cared about the community. Everyone who looked at Hester burned the pain of shame into her breast. Every whisper left her with an empty feeling in her stomach and a blush on her face. Even strangers and people she did not know personally caused her pain because they too were somehow part of the community. By looking at her, they branded her anew.

The Reverend Dinnesdale, her partner, suffered no less than Hester, but he suffered from guilt rather than shame. His pain came from within, starting and stopping within the perimeters of his personality. For poor Dinnesdale, however, this was no consolation. His guilt was so painful that it drove him to exposure and shame for relief. We can understand this, for we too feel driven to divulge or to confess our guilt. Unlike dogs, we human beings are willing to accept some bad consequences or punishment in order to relieve the unpleasant feeling of guilt. There is a little Dinnesdale in all of us.

On the other hand, Hester during her travail sought out privacy and the relief which came from withdrawing from public view.

The *Scarlet Letter* story shows the power and intrusiveness of a tight community sharing religious meanings, and in reaction to this intrusiveness many secular people have abandoned religious affiliation. For a while a least they glory in the freedom and anonymity of separate and anonymous existence. As time goes by, however, they realize that they have replaced one extreme with another without ever finding the middle course. People need community, shared meanings, and shared values. There are times when people ought to be ashamed. Some sense of community honor provides a strong motivation for honorable behavior. Without a concern about dishonor and disgrace, many awful, community-destroying misdeeds take place.

Ethnic groups maintain a sense of shame because they keep a sense of community alive. Irish Catholics, for example, talk about shame and scandalizing the outsider. Jews have a powerful word, *shandah*, and when they say, "for *shandah*," they mean something really disgraceful. People who don't care whether God or man looks at them or sees the things they do to others have no shame but are not better off by any means. They are pitiful and impoverished human beings. We have no reason to be ashamed of feeling shame. Both shame and pride guide our better selves.

But can the same be said for guilt? Who would dare say a kind word about guilt?

One of the characteristics of much of modern secular psychology is the rejection of guilt as unhealthy. Religion, for example, is dismissed out of hand on only one bit of evidence: it creates guilt. That seems to be sufficient, so strong is the assumption that guilt is something bad.

Avoiding guilt is as important in our secular culture as avoiding sin was in more religious times. Representatives of the new sciences are frequently called upon to help relieve a person of his guilt. A friend recently told me that he was seeing a psychiatrist because he felt guilty about leaving his wife. He paid top dollar to be assured that he had nothing to feel guilty about. Now he is relieved of that burden and said that he felt much happier.

Is guilt all that bad? Can guilt be so devoid of saving features that it is always to be avoided or relieved? Would the same psychiatrist whom my friend saw try to reassure a person who had perjured himself or stolen, or ruined someone's reputation by lying about them?

After all, only human beings can feel guilty, and those who do not feel guilt after doing wrong or hurtful things are less than human rather than more healthy. To be entirely incapable of this emotion is to qualify as a psychopath. Rather than being considered something evil, guilt should be recognized as something good: a humanizing sentiment which enhances man's capacity to live decently in society by discouraging his disruptive and destructive tendencies.

The human person stands alone in his capacity to distinguish those of his actions that should be approved from others that merit only disapproval. Man's conscience not only distinguishes good from bad behavior, but condemns what fails to come up to proper standards. Not just acts but omissions, not just decisions, but failure to decide, even wishes, can meet with condemnation.

Man can put even his acts at a certain distance from himself; he can reflect upon them and then either confirm or condemn them. Not only is guilt a uniquely human capability, but it serves a crucial social function. Guilt supplies an important counterforce to behaviors that are destructive of self and human community. Without this internal tribunal, truly human life would be threatened.

I know how much pain and suffering guilt has caused. I know that the capacity of guilt has been overworked by unloving parents to the enduring detriment of the child. And I know that religion has often been twisted and distorted by ministers, priests, and rabbis, who used the power of clergy to become moralistic bully boys, creating unnecessary guilt while acting out their hostility and vengeance.

But if guilt has been misused and abused, does this mean that the feeling has no value or no place in human life? Is there not a proper place for guilt, just as there is obviously improper and exaggerated guilt?

Guilt feelings following wrongful and hurtful actions lead to repentance and a commitment to change. Behavioral scientists who would do away with guilt would impoverish the human rather than enhance it.

In the past, symptoms were mistakenly treated as sins, and sick people were made to feel guilty. Today there are instances of sins being treated as symptoms, and people who should feel guilty are turned into patients.

But there is such a thing as excessive guilt or inappropriate guilt. Guilt is not always healthy. The old textbooks for confessors gave quite a bit of space to scrupulosity, a form of exaggerated guilt which required a lot of delicate attention in order to avoid making things worse. Perhaps the best defense against unhealthy guilt is to understand what kind of feeling it is and how best to manage it when it makes an appearance.

Trying to describe the feeling of guilt is difficult, because it is something like putting oneself on trial. Guilt follows an assessment of our behavior as deficient. Like a judge, guilt pronounces a condemnation, and it inflicts a punishment. To feel guilty is to be aware of being incriminated by an internal tribunal. Sometimes we are our own accusers. Or some other may call to our attention a bad behavior.

Following the accusation, there is a feeling like shame that causes us to blush deep down in our souls. Next may come an agitation or a heavy heart. All these feelings are so unpleasant that not infrequently we try to substitute anger for guilt, or we blame someone else, trying to shift the guilt to them. "If it weren't for you, damn it, I would not have done that." "You and your damn insistence on this or that." These statements are instances of an attempt to shift the blame to others after we have done something we are not proud of. Some people would rather take a beating than suffer the pain of feeling guilty.

There is no doubt that guilt is painful, but the pain of guilt is not useless. Unless we are victims of scrupulosity or have an exaggerated sense of wrongdoing, the guilt we feel is probably realistic, and the unpleasantness of the emotion if properly managed provides the push to move us toward behaviors that will reestablish the relationships disturbed by acts of selfishness, thoughtlessness, or cruelty.

What we do to manage guilt in a healthy way shows us the survival value of this feeling. Healthy guilt leads to expressions of regret which heal disrupted relations. And even more important than regret or contrition is the resolve to change which guilt can generate. "I'm just not going to do that again," or "I'm going to go out of my way to do something nice for. . . ," or, "Tonight I'm going to forget myself and give all my attention to. . . ."

If there are devices and impulses which work against the good of persons by destroying that necessary human community, guilt provides a crucial counter-balance. It is a very private feeling which does not show itself socially the way anger and fear do, but nevertheless has a distinct social function.

Who needs guilt? We do—if we want to live with others in something better than open warfare and aggression.

7. *Feeling angry*

Some people are angry so infrequently that they literally have to search their memories for the last time they had such an experience. Others are almost always angry. Hardly a day passes when they do not "fly off the handle." There are wide variations in individual lives, but everyone understands the word anger and does so by reference to personal experience.

What is it that we all understand? What is the structure of this very common and altogether human experience?

Anger arises out of situations in which a person experiences inability. In some cases the inability or powerlessness is one's own or resides in our very person. In other cases it is something outside that is unabling because it will not work or function as it should. Things that are expected to help us actually become obstacles, deskilling us and consequently making us angry.

If it is another person rather than a thing that constitutes an obstacle and causes anger, that person must be someone important: a parent, a brother or sister, an authority, a friend. People whom we do not care about or who mean nothing to us do not make us angry. When the other person is not important or the inability caused is not serious, we get feelings of impatience or aggravation. Anger, however, is reserved for serious frustration with an important other.

The experience of inability frustrates man, who is by nature active, an animal with goals and objectives to accomplish. In response to this frustration the body stiffens up and becomes tense. If the inability is serious, the tension can become downright explosive. The resulting behavior tends to be directionless, atypical, and usually ineffective in moving things or changing people. The unabling other tends to lose his or her usual qualities (friend, parent, boss) and becomes simply the one who is standing in the way. Anger destroys ordinary relationships. It mobilizes the body for aggression as fear mobilizes it for flight.

A spontaneous explosion or bursting forth is frequently prevented by all kinds of personal and social restrictions. To maintain a human community and social well-being, angry outburst must be controlled; so every society has norms governing such behavior. The severity of the norms is related to the status of the other person and the character of the interpersonal relationship. Asking for a reason, for example, is a suggested alternative to bodily explosion; but if it fails, then the person experiences a strong urge to vent destructive force on the things or persons who cause him to feel inability. The destructiveness may be direct and physical or it may take the slightly sublimated form of abusive language.

If the body tension is given direct physical expression, the angry feelings usually abate. If, however, the explosive bodily feeling is repressed or controlled, it often creates harmful and unpleasant experiences like muscle tightness, lack of coordination, headaches, stomach knotting, and overheating. Unable to be effective, human beings become affective in an angry mode.

A number of strategies tend to help in this unpleasant and threatening circumstance. Getting away from the frustrating situation is one of the best techniques. Either physical distance, or psychic distance created by doing something else that is enjoyable, or the intellectual distance brought about by reflection, all can be effective in moderating the explosive bodily feelings. The remedy of distance shows the extent to which anger involves a closeness to the situation in which we are trying to get something done.

Overinvolvement is balanced by some form of moving away, but distancing is not always so easy to accomplish. The person who makes us unable may be a spouse or family member from whom we cannot get far enough away. Sometimes anger can be changed only by a change in the other person.

Anger shows us that human beings are meant to be effective in getting things done and changing the world. Only when these constructive initiatives are frustrated does the body respond in explosive, expensive, and ineffective behaviors.

To be human then means to be able. Those who are frequently unable are frequently angry. Anger emerges out of a pragmatic dialogue between the person and the world. Understanding ourselves and our world a little better may help us control our angry explosions.

One thing is sure, we cannot consistently accomplish or always meet our goals. The conditions that generate anger will always be with us.

8. Feeling Useless

Ever since I was a small child I have been touched and saddened by blindness. Even today I get the same feelings I had as a child when I came across a blind person. I feel pity and want to help, and then I feel a little guilty at having such a gift as sight and not appreciating it. "How could I complain?" I think to myself. "How petty I am and how ungrateful, and how unappreciative of life's many unusual experiences." And then the thought process moves to another level of inquiry: "Why does God permit such evil as blindness? Why does he impose such a burden on people? How can these blind people be so strong and have such positive and happy attitudes?"

After so many years of living and thinking, I am finally beginning to make some sense of this mystery. I don't know anything more about the mystery of evil or God's will, but now I understand that those to be pitied are not the blind, but the sighted who have not accomplished anything with their lives. The real human tragedy is not blindness, but uselessness. The real loss is not sight, but self-esteem.

The human person has to do something significant with his life, or life will become an unbearable drudgery and an unrelenting humiliation. Depression is one of the most common painful consequences of a sense that one's life is going by and nothing is being accomplished. Without accomplishment there is no self-esteem, and consequently no happiness; even life's most intense pleasures have a bitter quality.

What type accomplishment is required for esteem and happiness? There are the unusual accomplishments of the world leader or a great novelist. Or there are the ordinary but very substantial accomplishments of running a home and raising a family. A father and mother have done something significant and receive recognition of this accomplishment in the reduced world of the family. This ordinary accomplishment constitutes great significance and self-esteem. "When I walk into the house and the children run to greet me, I'm king." Without significance and self-esteem, a person is condemned to a killing sadness.

Just how all these factors work out in life is illustrated in the story of a blind man who, after fifty-two years of darkness, completely recovered his sight. A happy story? Another testimony to the benefits of modern medicine? We'll see.

It took place in England in 1958. The man had been blind from the age of ten months as a result of an eye infection. Within hours after being operated on, the bandages were removed. First he saw the doctor's face. Then he moved about the hospital room, recognizing things like clocks and furniture. The same person who for years made his way by feeling, suddenly engaged in all the activities of the normally sighted person. It seemed miraculous.

Can't you just imagine Sam (we'll call him) moving from one new experience to another in an orgy of visual delight? A sunset, mountains, stars, moon, ocean, art, cities, children playing, and blooming flowers. Can't you imagine this man living out his life in joyful celebration after receiving what he had been deprived of for so long?

But it didn't happen. As a matter of fact, a little over a year after his operation Sam died of that killer emotional illness, depression.

During his fifty-two years as a blind man, he lived with high energy, interest in life, confidence, hope, and enthusiasm. Within a year after receiving his sight, he lost all these basic life ingredients. Depression robbed him of life in a way blindness never did.

As a blind man he had developed self-respect by accomplishing something significant without the benefit of sight. He had overcome a great obstacle. He had become a very good shoe repairman despite his handicap, and people admired him for what he had accomplished.

After receiving his sight, these previously remarkable achievements became undistinguished, ordinary, and even banal. Where before he was somebody, now he was like everyone else. Without his former accomplishments and self-esteem, depression colored the world more strongly than sight, and the color was black. Once depressed, everything he saw disappointed him.

I still thank God for sight and fear blindness, but I see the blind person somewhat differently now.

9. Feeling Worried

For the careful observer, our language tells us a lot about ourselves. There are instances, in fact, in which the way we speak about ourselves goes beyond description and reveals something of the elusive structure of our human condition.

Take, for example, the simple phrase "to worry oneself." "Don't worry yourself," we tell an anguished friend. "Why am I worrying myself?" is a criticism we often direct against ourselves. In these phrases our language gives us away as self-tormentors. When we take a careful look we are forced to admit that in many cases we are our own worst enemy. Our thoughts put us in a kind of prison, and both our attempts to get out and our complaints about confinement tend only to tighten the chains.

The self-torment of worry is like a persistent weed in the garden of life which flourishes in the soil of inactivity. The active person, energetically pursuing some goal, is immunized against this painful disorder. Worry, for example, can keep a person from sleeping, and insomnia provides just the inactivity which in turn intensifies worry. Lying there doing nothing invites in the fears and uncertainties which ordinarily are kept contained by activity and accomplishment. If we were able to test the insomniac we would find that he gets more sleep than he thinks, but the debilitating exhaustion he feels after a restless night is real. He feels shot down because he has been torturing himself half the night with worry.

Work, on the other hand, constitutes a healthy activity. It is a shame that totalitarian regimes have by their work camps and forced labor given the concept of work as therapy such a black eye. Hidden beneath the many inhumanities of forced labor is a very human truth; i.e., that work is health-creating. One of the shames of our mental-health institutions is a prohibition against requiring the patient to work. Consequently, thousands of poor souls who were worried to death to start with sit around all day with nothing to do but worry. It is

when a person no longer responds to the demands for work
that he loses power and succumbs to the ravishes of inactivity. Just look at the once-proud worker forced by an un-
wanted retirement to sit and disintegrate under the influence
of petty self-inflicted torments. The worrier is estranged from
his better and more powerful self.

Why then doesn't the worrier get up and get going? Why
doesn't he find some satisfying and productive work which
would occupy him, engage his mind creatively, and consequently make him much happier? There are many reasons,
but the one we find most frequently is a loss of trust and self-
confidence. The worrier sits and torments himself because he
distrusts his own powers. Such distrust of oneself leads
quickly to distrust of others. And gradually the prison closes
in.

A description of worry easily takes on a moral tone—one
which condemns the worrier. Just as inactivity cannot be confused with modesty or humility, it cannot be identified either
with laziness or immorality. Distrust of oneself and others is
rooted in some deprivation or loss very early in childhood
over which the sufferer had little control and for which he is
certainly not responsible. To learn to trust oneself and others
is the first and most basic emotional acquisition that comes
from a protective and nourishing environment (good enough
mothering) and not from anything the baby can do for himself. Rather than being condemned then, the worrier merits
our understanding. Everything possible must be done to help
the worrier recover—at whatever late date—the all-important
trust from which activity can flow.

Here we return to our language and what it says about us.
If man is a being who worries himself and undermines himself, he is also the being who can turn himself around. Our

language also includes reflexive verbs like "to activate oneself" and "to trust oneself." Again, language reveals the underlying structure of the human being.

Moving from the self-torment of worry, however, to self-actualization and self-trust is never easy. The great sages from earliest times have tried to help man control his self-defeating thoughts, but it is tough for the worrier to take the first step away from his painful habit of self-torment. And the advice he or she usually gets from friends is likely to do more harm than good.

"Worrying doesn't help" is a bit of good advice everyone gives on occasion. "Stop worrying" is another of those helpful commands we issue to friends when we spot their furrowed brow and glum manner.

We give advice and injunctions to others, but there is no one in his right mind who can say, "Look at me—I don't worry." Alfred Newman of *Mad* magazine ("What, me worry?") gets by purely on the basis of his deficient humanness.

Why do we worry anyway? For the simple reason that worry goes with the human condition. It is not something peculiar to parents or old people and non-existent in children. Human beings at every age have their worries. Managing life to a great extent depends upon a person's success in managing worry.

Little children worry about mean dogs, or losing their parents. Teenagers worry about their bodies, their looks, their peers. College students worry about courses, careers, and relationships. As we get older we don't stop worrying, but rather just experience a change in what we worry about. There is always something.

Some of the reasons for worrying are obvious: mean dogs threaten a child's security; peer opinion threatens an adolescent's fragile identity; college courses involve judgments and the possibility of failure which is always threatening. In each case worry centers around a person's sense of self-esteem.

But why is self-esteem so great a problem? Why is it so vulnerable? Why so open to doubt? These questions go to the root of man's paradoxical situation.

Even the small child has a need to be recognized as special. The self is not content to be just a self. It insists upon being significant. And yet the specialness and the significance is not given or automatic. Rather it has to be created. Each human being has a deep-seated need to be recognized as significant and realizes at the same time that it is up to him to create his own significance.

To satisfy his drive to stand out, a person must expose himself to many kinds of threats. Standing out means being different, becoming an individual, standing alone, abandoning the power and support of family, and all these actions involve risk.

On the one hand a person senses a drive for individuality and on the other hand the terror of being an individual. Unless the person creates his own significant self, it will never come to be, and yet the act of self-creation is difficult and full of danger. It requires overwhelming strength. Only God creates with ease.

Faced with such a threatening life task, the human being responds with a great deal of thinking, rethinking, fretting, pacing, and brow furrowing with worry. If the person takes any step at all in the direction of creating a significant self it is preceded by worry. And if no step is taken, there is even more worry about not being able to meet life's demands. Since the creation of a significant self is a never-ending project, the accompanying worry is always with us.

All worry is ultimately worry about self and self-esteem. It might seem that we are worrying about something outside, but really we are worried about our own self. The most significant selves with the healthiest self-esteem worry but manage to move beyond their worry to self-affirming acts. Those of us who are pitiful, worry and do not act. To save ourselves from threats we silently retreat only to die a thousand deaths and in addition to be consumed with worry.

Instructions like "Don't worry" are usually issued with all the good will in the world but they never help. They do nothing to relieve the inner doubt or to strengthen the fragile sense of self.

Who ever said life was easy? Especially for the person without outstanding gifts or powers, measuring up to life's demands requires enormous and persistent courage. Just managing to keep worry sufficiently under control to perform an occasional self-affirming act is itself a form of heroism.

10. Feeling Bored

Every culture contributes something to human beings who participate in it, and at the same time distorts and limits the participants. Because each person tends to see his own culture as natural or normal, its influence is generally unnoticed. Only a privileged few have the opportunity to live in different parts of the world and to have different experiences which provide them with a clearer perspective on their own culture. Most people have little against which to compare their culture and its influence on them.

One aspect of our culture that is generalized and painful, and yet very much ignored, is the feeling of boredom. In the Middle Ages, writers and preachers gave a lot of attention to this condition. There were a number of different words for boredom, which was feared both as sinful and dehumanizing.

One term, *abulia,* is still around in psychiatric vocabulary and means an inability to take action or a lack of willpower.

In medieval culture, the bored person was in danger of losing his direction in life. Having goals which created energy and generated activity was believed then to be of capital importance for earthly success or other-worldly salvation. To be bored was to be aimless and directionless, uninvolved and inactive in the all-important struggle of life. *Acedia*, another word for boredom, was considered both a grave sin and a grave vital danger. The church, which then was the agent both of mental health and salvation, preached often against the influence of this potentially destructive feeling. Talk in confessionals often centered on the issues of boredom and the richness of words for this condition reflects this interest in the topic. Associated terms include: sloth, indifference, laziness, callousness, apathy.

Today's preachers do not often touch this theme, and one sees little about it even in professional psychological literature. And yet boredom seems to be more of a problem for us than it was in medieval culture. Many teenagers today, for example, seem always to be bored. There is never anything to do. Nothing is interesting, nothing is worth striving for. As a result, rather than being energized by immediate and long-term goals, life is experienced as a drag. Without something to strive for, life itself becomes a burden. Drugs become a costly and ineffective remedy for this unpleasant feeling. And teenagers are not the only examples—just the best. Boredom permeates every age group in our culture. It affects both the "cultured" and those who consider the cultured to be snobs.

The bored person may look relaxed or laid back, but there is a big difference between the two conditions. Relaxation is enjoyable and reconstitutes the person to engage in creative pursuits. Boredom, on the other hand, is painful and does nothing for creativity. The French word for boredom is *ennui*, and it carries all the negative connotations we have discussed along with loneliness, weariness, and annoyance. In German, *langeweile* conveys the notion of painful awareness of time. Bored people "kill time." And if we consider the importance of time for human beings, we notice the self-destructive and dehumanizing aspect of boredom.

It does not seem accidental that so many people in our culture seek relief for their pained existence in drugs which ultimately put a person to sleep. Drug preference reflects the problems being medicated and the most commonly used drugs today have sedative effects. If there is nothing worthwhile doing, it hardly makes sense to increase one's activity. For the bored person, existence is heavy; there are no values; it makes no difference what happens, so why not just nod off. No wonder the medieval thinkers thought this mood to be so dangerous.

The mystery is why contemporary thinkers do not pay more attention to this feeling. After all, it didn't disappear with medieval culture or the practice of going to confession. It is more pervasive today than ever before. In fact, it may be the one feeling that has to be revealed to contemporary persons. Since almost everyone is somewhat bored, boredom can easily be taken to be the normal state of affairs in this culture and consequently ignored.

Ignorance, however, is always costly. Boredom is a feeling that needs to be recognized for what it is in order to be relieved. And there are different types of boredom that must be recognized as well. Anyone can be bored with a book or a movie or a conversation, and such boredom is of little consequence. When, however, a person is not bored with some thing or outside object but with his or her own self, then something much more serious has developed. The typical materialistic American who moves from one experience to the next, from one place to another, from one pleasure, one woman, one job to another in pursuit of variety and freedom is not only bored but likely not to realize the seriousness of his or her condition. Boredom with oneself, experienced perhaps as emptiness or depression, is commonplace.

The standard solution is to move to still more varieties of experience for relief. Bored with the country, one moves to the city, or vice versa. If the United States is boring, why not take a trip to some foreign country. Search for relief involves endless moving and changing but without finding real help. Modern people find plenty of distractions, but looking closely one can notice a lot of only superficial mirth. Real gratification costs more and more time and effort until the moving and the endless rounds of distractions collapse of their own excessive weight. Then even modern man suffers *abulia*, in the sense of an inability to take meaningful action or to exercise real initiative. And *acedia*, in the sense of aimlessness, takes the place of direction in life. Life then is characterized by the weariness of *ennui* and the time-consciousness of *langeweile*.

This may be the saddest of all the feelings and the one most in need of thoughtful awareness in order to be avoided. Where there is a sense of self that needs to be rescued from threatening forces, mistakes may be made in the selection of coping devices, but at least there is energy, drive, and the will to correct the selection. Boredom, however, saps life. It destroys the very sense of self and creates a kind of living death. Ultimately all emotional illness reflects a preference for death. The real issue for each of us is the choice of life in the face of death.

So, at last, we have come to the end of this exercise, and

endings are always associated with fear. Will what I have written make a book? Will the book be published? Will it sell? If it gets attention, will critics tear it apart? There are reasons to be afraid. If I was at the beginning rather than at the end, I would have tried to do things differently. I would, for example, like to have created a few laughs, and I know that I didn't even come close. Ending up with a reflection on boredom, I can't help thinking, "My God, I didn't relieve boredom, but only added to it."

The Protestant tradition is based on the insight that failure, faults, and sin accompany every human effort. The insistence upon sin and failure may seem dour to Catholics whose tradition emphasizes the goodness of God's creation. But, as we might expect, the two traditions need each other, and both together combine to provide the best of all help for managing life and life's feelings. Belief in a God who forgives our faults and failures and the use of prayer to avail oneself of that forgiveness are the best therapy for much of life's unpleasantness. Once forgiven, then joy and all the other positive feelings can flow more naturally. Celebrating belongs both to religion and therapy.

NOTES

I. UNDERSTANDING HUMAN FEELINGS

1. Menninger, Karl, *The Human Mind* (New York, Knopf, 1973) p. 3.

2. Butler, Samuel, *The Way of All Flesh* (New York, Dutton, 1903) Quoted by Karl Menninger in *The Vital Balance* (New York, Viking, 1975).

3. The personality disorders include: 1) Passive Aggressive Personality, 2) Obsessive Compulsive Personality, 3) Hysterical Personality, 4) Explosive Personality, 5) Asthenic Personality, 6) Inadequate Personality, 7) Schizoid Personality, 8) Cyclothmic Personality, 9) Paranoid Personality, 10) Antisocial Personality. Sexual Deviance and Alcohol/Drug Dependence are also included under personality disturbances.

4. The psychiatric categories frequently used today to refer to this type personality are "psychophysiologic disorder," and "somatization reactions."

II. LEVELS OF HEALTHY AND UNHEALTHY FUNCTIONING

1. Menninger, Karl, *The Vital Balance* (New York: Viking, 1963).

2. I am leaving out of consideration the issue of euthanasia, which is a form of suicide aided by medical personnel. There are extreme cases in which a patient who is in the dying process and in intractable pain may reasonably choose to die.